DAVID KINLOCH

Finger of a Frenchman

CARCANET

First published in Great Britain in 2011 by
Carcanet Press Limited
Alliance House
Cross Street
Manchester M2 7AQ

A CIP catalogue record for this book is available from the British Library

ISBN 978 1 84777 074 5

The author acknowledges support for this project from the Scottish Arts Council
and from the Arts and Humanities Research Council (AHRC).

Arts & Humanities
Research Council

The publisher acknowledges financial assistance from Arts Council England

Supported by
ARTS COUNCIL
ENGLAND

Typeset by XL Publishing Services, Tiverton
Printed and bound in England by SRP Ltd, Exeter

Finger of a Frenchman

DAVID KINLOCH was born, raised and educated in Glasgow. He is a graduate of the universities of Glasgow and Oxford and was for many years a teacher of French studies. He currently teaches creative writing and Scottish literature at the University of Strathclyde, Glasgow. He is the author of four previous collections including *Un Tour d'Ecosse* (2001) and *In My Father's House* (2005), both published by Carcanet, and of many critical works in the fields of French, Translation and Scottish studies. In 2004 he was a winner of the Robert Louis Stevenson Memorial Award and in 2006 held a Scottish Writers' Bursary from the Scottish Arts Council. He was a founder editor of the poetry magazine *Verse* and has been instrumental in setting up the first Scottish Writers' Centre.

For Mum

Acknowledgements

Thanks are due to the editors of the following magazines and journals where some of these poems first appeared: *The Dark Horse, Ecloga, International Literary Quarterly, New Writing: The International Journal for the Theory and Practice of Creative Writing, Orbis, PN Review, Painted, Spoken, Poetry International Web, Poetry Review, PS, The Scottish Review of Books, The Journal of Stevenson Studies, The Journal of Irish and Scottish Studies.*

'The Organ Bath' first appeared in *Contemporary Poetry and Contemporary Science*, edited by Robert Crawford (Oxford: Oxford University Press, 2006). 'Three Gaelic Versions' first appeared in *Dreuchd an fhigheadair: The Weaver's Task: A Gaelic Sampler*, edited and introduced by Crìsdean MhicGhilleBhàin (Edinburgh: Scottish Poetry Library, 2007). 'The Mocking Fairy' was commissioned by the Glasgow Mirrorball network of poets to mark the lifetime achievement of the Scottish artist, Hannah Frank.

The sequence of poems about paintings that forms the core of this collection was made possible by the award of a Writers' Bursary from the Scottish Arts Council and a research grant from the Arts and Humanities Research Council. I am grateful for both of these. Many people showed me great kindness during the course of this project, including many archivists, librarians, gallery keepers and owners and I should like to thank them all. In particular, I should like to mention Kenneth Dunn who went out of his way to make my task easier at the National Library of Scotland. Morven Gregor introduced me to the work of T.J. Clark. I owe a debt of gratitude also to my colleagues at the University of Strathclyde for allowing me the time necessary to complete this book. I thank Richard Price, Gerry McGrath and Donny O'Rourke for their poetic camaraderie and useful advice, and Eric for his uncomplaining patience.

Once

Once, he dreamt of the road not taken: crashing
in panic through undergrowth to reach it, crossing
the forbidden gardens of big houses, staving
his foot on the wishing stile, then
suddenly, he turned a familiar corner
and the street began to climb: he stopped
before a ship-shaped villa and saw him
through the window, sitting calmly,
his brown eyes fixed on a book or cards

at just that moment, a single phrase of music
played from a space beside the bed;
he seemed to wake and layed his arm
across the body of another;
together they listened to the silence
then rose and began the day.

Contents

Small Pleasures

Five Portraits of Mary

Mary Stuart's Dream

Reine de France Marie
'Quatrain', Mary, Queen of Scots

When I sit late at works, almost
within the verdure of this tower's
only tapestry – rabbits in an orange tree
by my shoulder – an old globe
chases silly latitudes beneath
the casement window and looking out,
the scant, dank countryside makes up
fields of Poitou mist. Distantly at first,
– but the globe birls it closer – a giant
oak shaped like a country crests
towards my berth. A man wreathed
in raindrops disembarks. Do the King's
swans flee him? Is that cry a peacock
at midday? I hear his feet discreetly
pad the pockmarked steps and now
he is before me. Alone. With his box
of little instruments. He is a humble man
and the Scots leid on his lips is just
the burr that made my cradle sleepy.
Together we compare our cabinet of works:
my *petit point*, his burin, my panels
of darned net, his tiny hammers,
chalk and chisels, a balletic compass
to take the measure of my smile.
I laugh and show him coins aplenty:
billons, testoons emblazoned with my features
and the King's, French treasure of our large
estates and mottos, trees of Jesse, crosses,
fleurs de lys and lion rampant. Poor man!
His journey has been fruitless. And yet
he shields his eyes against my two poor
candles and beckons me down the cold
stone steps towards his ship quoting
Leonardo: 'In the streets at twilight, Madam,

note the faces of men and women
when the weather is bad, how much attractiveness
is seen in them.' He will draw me,
draw me into the haar which lies on
this strange country like a mourning veil.
I nod above my embroidery, start awake
and hunt for my jewelled casket,
feverishly fingering small change
for the evidence of my head.

La Monnaie du Moulin

She moved swiftly on her accession:
commands me give my drawing of her head
to the new coin millers on the City's island
next to Notre Dame. An odd workshop:
unnaturally quiet, only the whoosh
of pendulum and click of balance
wheel filtering the silver rush. Few men.
Automated imprints of a royal will.
She loves the promise of geometry,
perfect circles for Divine Right
and wants each coined head to weigh
the same, induce at last an impossible
equality among her peoples. The effigy
that just says 'monarch' is *vieux jeu*
now we have the means to show a living
likeness of this Scottish queen to subjects
of three kingdoms she lays claim to.
She craves true fame, not just title
and dominion, waves aside my mild
objection that, hitherto, majesty discreetly
veiled, a little distant, has benefited all
thrones. 'No, Sir. Your skill at chiaroscuro
betrays you. Shadow as though it were not
shadowed is best shadowed for the modern
monarch. Draw me in sunlight, always.'
I bowed. Except the engravers' guilds
won't wear it, down tools and picket

La Monnaie du Moulin, lament the loss
of art such sleight of hand entails;
hands useless now, laid off, quite
hammerless. I see both points of view
because I am a stranger and a simple
portraitist. Coloured chalk's my medium:
easily erased, begun again if sovereigns
don't fancy too much light. I play
for time: the weak boy king trails
in her wake of wrist frills and snaking
curls. He won't outlive the strike
and Mary may return to Scotland
where they can't make out the detail
on their coins through fogs of dull
theocracy. She'll have no French head.
Scottish? And England: that's the stuff
of dream or nightmare. I have to weigh
the risks you see: a majesty's displeasure
or the boycott of good clients, my friends
the chisellers, the hammerers, so soon
to be of yore. Perhaps I could be broker
to a deal: the guilds may keep the heads
of kings and queens, slough off
their rage at poverty by beating them – as usual –
to desired consistency; but the little coins,
coins of the little people will be struck mechanically:
billons of small worth, the silver sunk in copper
until it cannot shine and scattered
with dark marks of provenance,
dates and mottoes. A fair exchange?
The master guildsmen think so.
But if I have betrayed them – and I have –
it is to win them surely a larger kingdom
at a later date. I know economy:
greater quantities of surer coins,
however small their value, will ground
a growing bourgeoisie, increase
the common people's power.
And so the need for louis d'or
to take the place of mounds of change

that hole the pockets of new furred gowns
will tip too far the balance I have struck
and great ones' heads fall at last
within the purview of the miller's guillotine.

A Coin

for Edwin Morgan

John Acheson struck me. Master of the Mint,
he was engraver to the Medicis and the Scottish queen
whose portrait he dug hard for in my golden flesh.
His hands twisted out the corkscrew curls,
scraped the swan-like neck for heads,
lion rampants for my tails. I've aged with her,
my high colour burnished, though still
I offer her an image of her profile on the brink
of greatness: Great Queen of France and Scots
and England, her crown both regal and the tiara
of her Roman faith. Tip me to certain angles
in the sunlight and you'll catch reflections
of Chambord afternoons and at night a glimmer
of the candles ranked and raked on ballroom floors.
I announced a Golden Age and she has used me well
to pay off poets, artists, murderers
though each was just by proxy.
Her time dwindles now but I am constant.
Save once: when someone threw me in a pond
of goldfish for good luck. I sank
and as the water's fingers stroked my rim,
the sacred profile that I carry wavered
in the shallows as if struck clumsily
in another age or country, peered
helplessly through weird vegetation,
mirk, mist, and for a moment I seemed to mark
a different story, crossed by dark shapes
I did not recognise. One of the Maries
fished me out, restored me to that brilliant reign.
Although to do so went against a powerful wish.

Fotheringay, 1587

If I could cast out
               the net of *lacis*
from the tower window
                       gather up the frilled pinks
and columbines swimming
                   upstream
to the juniper…

'It is all distant enough
to look embroidered.'

Pearl of water. Not
pearl, no
but how the hinge of oiled pebbles
opens
the river's silver inlay to itself.

Look! There is the silly rabbit of life
hopping   hopping

My voice is the unicorn
in a mirror: inaudible
castrato.

It is the damp
suggests our subjects:
sneiles
a sea moonke
a she Dolphin fische.
(Trust not overmuch
in appearance.)

The seven planets
in *petit point*
enriched with gold and silver.
The North Star

not completed

Family

When the axe fell in Fotheringay:
once – not quite – twice,
the art began:

Catholic courts commanded
ikon after ikon
and among them this:

a tiny Mary Stuart
wrought in ivory
whose skirts spring open
to reveal beneath carved awnings
her son and cousin
complete with orb and sceptre,
a frame to the famous scene of martyrdom,
central to the triptych.

Cut in Venice
for a Croatian bishop,
she took ship for Korkula
and as she crested Adriatic waves
the little warring family
pushed out from her womb of skirts
to claim the filigree of passing
islands, the lace of limestone peninsulae,
cleansed, walled cities,
small nations pared as whittled ivory.

Resisting Hell

i.m. Esther Inglis, calligrapher, 1571–1624

I

Victorious and venerable King, most virtuous scholar,
I, Esther Inglis, calligrapher, humbly send this tiny buik of
Valediction. My husband – who once spied for you – bears final
Envoi. It is written in a hand called Death and hails from

Leith, a town I etch within triangular serifs
And a trembling line. Its smoke curls up initial capitals, ignites

Preface, this epistle which crawls immaculately to you, High
Lord of Scots, of England, France; we both enjoy the tribute of our
Underlings: mine are these poems in my praise by Kinloch,
Melville, references stitched up in Latin and pasted in for
Esther, 'paragon and matchless mistress of the golden pen'.

II

Recovering the spirit of 'ane Amazon',
Esther stipples an oval ground of cobalt blue.
She seats herself in front of sheet music, quill and ink,
Inscribes her portraits complete with hats that say it all:
Some are smart and conical above a ruff, others low crowned,
Thumb Bible sized, picked from the rack of emblemata that
Inventory her life: here are leeks and monkeys, tassels and white urns;
Naomi, Sarah, Rebecca; Susanna, Hannah, Judith: no lady in a
Garden could be as patient, meek and brave as this medicinable
Hand, slippered in long gloves, herb script of *lettre pattée*, of *lettera*
                                                                    rognosa,
Easing out the periods of her silent race, the pinks and pansies of
                                                                    shamefastness.
Lord! Oh, my tottering right hand offers up one
Last velvet strawberry, this silky anagram:

ESTHER INGLIS RESISTING HELL

III

I dreamt that I was at my escritoire again:
dawn over Leith and Leith nestling in the curling
terminals I give the letter C of Christ our Lord.
And then I dreamt the tiny town spoke from the hand
they call *civilité*, cried out to Esther crouched
with her crow quill over bees and whirlpool motifs.
I dreamt that little people clinging to the roofs
or snug in the crow's nest of a cresting ship
spied how my lines of *lettera mancina*
undulate eternally from page to page.
I saw the people balance dizzily
and drown in a kaleidoscope of shapes.
I dreamt they screamed that they were trapped
in language and lonely, wrecked in a partial view:
a few red tiles, a single sail and then I felt
my forty different hands weigh down
my body like nights of wilderness.
I dreamt this flattened costal town
was all that I could get of life,
just several strokes of *chancery*
beneath grotesques and river goddesses.
And that my art was copied from the books of men.

To a Gentleman of the King's Bedchamber

Lovinge father from lovinge sonne:
beginning is no impediment even if
totters, starts and stops stud syntax;
end can be epiphany or void;
what vexes most: the deepest middle,
winds hanging as they do. Art
helps. I have a man who sends me
scenes and portraits: John Clerk
of Penicuick, merchant for me
au nom de Jesus sur le pont at Paris.

Lovinge father from lovinge sonne
I plod back home to them,
my family of pictures, fix my
Tintoretto at three hundred duckets
di banco firm in my mind, as prayers
fog middle distance, rheumy
flares that singe and curl to ash.
Preachers are in the fields, black
on knolls; there are action sermons
and I confess the solemn league and covenant.

Lovinge father from lovinge sonne:
I have begun a book of maxims:
it is surpassing dull. The sentences go:
'A man that hath', 'A man that hath not'.
It is the murky white between
that pulls me in, bone coloured ditches
where I sit and sit
and try and try. I make warre.
I pray. I keep estate. Separate seeming
men who each believe he is complete.

Lovinge father from lovinge sonne:
what is a petrified crayfish, a dried-up
chameleon, clay figures from the tombs of Egypt?
Gentlemen want picture galleries
despite the clerics' censure,
but I desire a room stacked high
with faces, windows on lives of others,
to find in one or two a semblance
of the other men I am; a sense of corridor
behind their backs where my souls might meet.

Lovinge father from lovinge sonne:
scattered boxes on the dock at Leith,
tobacco, spoons, one curious ivory whistle;
I tripped against a something full of holes
for draining water; there was a compass
and a turtle's long pink tooth. And then,
this double portrait: *Two Young Men*,
propped up against the poop
of Hamburg's ship as if they took
the east-coast morning air.

Lovinge father from lovinge sonne:
I did not buy them. Are they brothers?
Friends? Beneath an arch a man in black
offers an apple, stalk down, to one in red.
Black doublet smiles at us.
Red doublet smiles at him.
Look hard and you will see behind their backs
a bird with outstretched wings. A swan?
An eagle? On the right shoulder
of the apple-giving boy, an owl...

Lovinge father from lovinge sonne:
your letter to me once at Cambridge
said 'Follow your book.' I was obedient.
I gave my gentleman a signet ring
for my present business was my book;
father, loving father, what *is*
a gentleman of the bedchamber?
Perhaps our king sleeps precious little
in his warres with parliaments.
I did not bid for *Two Young Men*. It is

in Holland now, their place of birth,
with Charles's son, awaiting restoration.
But when I cannot sleep another owl cries out
and when I can there is a rush of wings;
a man in a quadrangle gilt with sun
hands me an apple and when I cut it
open there is a white and empty chamber:
I step inside and am your lordship's
most obedient, most lovinge sonne.

Rousseau on Ramsay

The pelisse? The furs? The hat?
The Armenian coat? At Ramsay's
suggestion? That king-copying coloniser?
My 'companion piece', Hume?
That turtle-eating, pensioned, imperial
alderman, tacitly propped up on Tacitus?
Hume, is that you in the mirror
on the opposite wall
where I can take you in at my ease?
Is that you, Hume, ready to patronise,
ready to shepherd me out of
or into the dark?
Why are my bowels so sunk in shadow?
To suggest – by inversion – my kidney
complaint? The drizzle of pee matting
the lining that hides a forked body?
Why is the light like an eye that
eats at my face, that pokes out my eyes
and makes me a Cyclops?
Why has he posed me – or did I request
it? – as in a self-portrait, half–
turned towards you? How dare
he confess me, place my frail finger
over my heart? My heart, my eyes?
Is this all there is of me? Is it to make me
easy to copy? So he can sell me like
'petits pains'? Can't he tie me together
or down with his daubs, see into the I,
his brush like the lace of memory
just touching and veiling a void?
Who gazes at me with such intensity?
Where am I? Hello? Out there,
you? Is that an 'aye' I can hear?
Hume, are you there? Or the artist even?
Is it evening now? Is it only I
that can answer these questions?

Young Blade

Moonlight becomes blades, blades moon-
light as they lilt and pivot out of shadow
into yellow pools: I make a point and stop:

steam breath into air that cracks like ice,
close eyes upon a world that gleams
and scrapes and rasps; 'Look out!'

Brown, behatted, a figure grasps
my arm and birls me about; I make a run:
circling to the centre of the loch –

cross stroke, chassé, cross over slip – turn
and look back across the white and shining
field: the huddle of 'ingénues'

practising their 8s, the cries of 'off!'
and 'change!', the silver scales
of safety ropes slithering from baskets;

silence set off by distant swish.

And so I see the scene again: late
afternoon; the little minister, still svelte
but on the verge of portliness, breasting
the ice with a frank and open stroke;

his friends, the painters, smiling, betting:
which one could lay down just that shade
of lilac shadow cast by the suburban
Mercury, silhouetted *contre jour*?

Then, the sudden hush as water tensed
at his instruction, trout gazed up at his incisive feet.
I felt that God must be in clarity like this
and listened to the valley echo

the striations of his silver blades.
Far out on Duddingston Loch
our true apostle sped with twice the speed
of Christ who walked on waves.

I saw him harrow ice with grace of the elect
and scar the transubstantiation
of wintered elements. At once I heard
a tapping from the hills

as if a tiny hammer big with work
sought to split this world: the shelf
of ice with all its merry skaters
cracked from side to side then tipped

like a sinking ship; loch made
meadow loch as little cows,
aristocratic blades, the Reverend
and his painters clung to trees

above a sundered castle, floated off
to villages, new towns, enlightened
schemes and sunken moonlit pastures.
With a sense of real presence

he crossed my vision: and I wondered
if it mattered which man would win
the bet: Raeburn or Danloux?

Both helped him to untie
the fine pink inkles strapping blade
to boot and walked away with him

arm in arm towards the village.

Sir David Wilkie Administering Tea in Kensington

'A Mr Delacroix to see you, Sir.
With a brace of partridges
and a very handsome turkey.'

There was chat: how gendarmes,
'Damned gendarmes' nicked
the Scot for sketching Calais gates;

how old Hogarth was beaten up,
deported for the same; linked arms
upon a sunlit lawn, strolling

towards talk of paint: *tête de negre*,
vert bronze; the Frenchman lost
in *fumée de Londres*;

the mere sound of a smile,
'Monsieur', stopped Géricault
from working; most shadow

contains violet: is there a recipe?
'Cassel earth, dear Sir' mixed
in with white. Gleams from a teapot

strike them on the tartan rug:
a housemaid tries to still
a storied platter, cakes

swinging to the motion of her walk
across the greensward,
steam and silver swaying

like a censer through the air;
a doll in the distance, the sloping
garden magnifies her step by step

until she spreads a tablecloth
of sacramental white,
stands beadle-like and pours:

'Macaroon or shortbread, Sir?'
Later, Wilkie bids her fetch
his 'shadow-box', a tiny Knox

carved out of clay, spirited
wings of his little cloak
flung out indignantly at the idol

the artist will make of him.
Delacroix smiles, recalls
small windmills on the angle

of a barn, automata
of a pint-sized coach and horses
that trundled through the Dauphin's childhood;

a large red butterfly settles
briefly on the head of Knox,
canopies the preaching toy

beneath a ruby shimmer.
The Frenchman laughs aloud
to see it sip and read the pulpit's book:

'Draw this my friend? It's worth
more than all our canvases.'
Wilkie gestures and falls

silent. Delacroix looks up,
is dazzled by the sun,
struggles to follow the fritter

of the butterfly among
the stars of History.
It dances out a crazy line

around the picnic party
and the artists – abashed –
allow the summer's day

to take their measure,
make them models
in this laboratory of space:

the maid, starched and glittering
with sugar spoons, the men's
heads, clear and dark as jewels,

the white cloth spread in quiet
communion, bodies on a rug
at just this   to each other.

Sleuth

1 The Company

18 May 1882, 5 p.m.

Mère Chevillon is at her *tisanes* again,
fussing over the Ullman boy. The distant clink
of tea-spoons on best china counterpoint
an evening filled with jackdaw cries,
the persistent jackass laughter of a plague
of ducks out on the River Loing that cuts off
the sloping garden of our inn. One is christened
'Caesar' and tonight I'd happily be his Brutus.
Ullman is ill, will die; here perhaps; we'll have
a little ceremony in our courtyard. O'Meara,
the Irishman, will speak – he always does –
of wasted youth, the confraternity of *plein air*
painters who'd found a fresh disciple
in the recently deceased. I can't be sad.
TB has done for him and he'll go out
with the soft Grez light he's mortgaged
everything to see, mourned by peers
who value him. And then he'll be replaced.
They rise like hoverflies from the riverbank
brush first; dishevelled, hot, smocks
sticky with willow, they cling to unlikely spots,
and hang from palettes by their thumbs,
clusters of them painting each other
painting views and the locals, none
of whom have time to stand and stare.
They smell of lavender and chew tobacco.
Who is here then? Foreigners with difficult
Anglo-Saxon, Swedish names: a Scot
called Melville, Stott of Oldham,
– wherever that may be – a genius: Carl
Larsson and a fellow-countryman,
small and tense with lots of hair
who thinks he's one as well: Strindberg
is his name. A Simeon Solomon – utterly

improbable – and my favourite: John Lavery,
compact, gregarious, with too much charm.
Listen: the tanned vowels of young men
gathered over beer tumble up to me;
gorgeous *saltimbanques* of laughter
peel briefly and jag as if mocking me
for being me and absent from the company.

2   The Art

21 May 1883, 4 p.m.

'Monsieur le Comte, I challenge you to a duel!'
His arched eyebrows, smile, accompanying
snigger of O'Meara and the rest suggested
a joke, a dare, another diversion
from the job of painting. Yet from the corner
of my eye I'd spied him at it, assiduous
for days before the canvas of a rower
with moustaches kissing hands at ladies
in *bateaux de plaisance* drifting past him.
The surface splendour of the oarsman's costume,
a classic striped affair, replied vivaciously
to the girls' parasols and the little sub-plot
danced among the sparkling greens and whites.
Perfect. A day of mischief, sunny *far niente*
summed up within a four franc gold leaf frame.
'Well, Comte Henri de Lestrange, will you play
our game? My painting versus your photography?'
I instantly demurred: we could not find
the dapper rower and the girls were back
in Paris no doubt. And then the whole
thing was to take the moment *sur le vif*,
upon the cusp of being there and gone.
A replay would betray respective arts.
Or some such stuff. He shrugged,
produced another painting: 'This one,
would be easier, *A Grey Summer's Day in Grez*.
You see?' It was more posed: a straw hatted
man – Lavery himself – with back to the spectator

gazes at the water. Nearby a woman sits
reading in a campaign chair. Stillness,
the minnows and the water lilies. Only
the greyhound, Fred, ears pricked,
looks down the path and is aware
of us, of me as I approach. I gave in.
Misgivings? Plenty. They wished 'to view
"The Silver Sunbeam"' as my camera is called,
snoop beneath my hood,
'observe the alchemist at work'.
In art they count my aristocracy
at nought. To them I am a peasant
drunk on new machinery, an artisan
before these grandees of oil and gouache.
Why humour them? Was it the friendliness
I seemed to find in Lavery's frank face?
I should have paid attention to the angle
of the shadow cast by the ruined tower
next door. It's called *La Tour de Ganne*
from Latin 'gannum' meaning trap,
betrayal, deception and derision.

9 p.m.

And so I raised him: Karin Bergöö,
Larsson's wife, sat sketching in a chair.
Lavery was himself, as was the Loing,
its coolness, light running up
the underside of leaves, ambulatory,
mechanical, mocking us at our outdoor
parlour game. The difficulty was Fred,
who did not want to play but flopped
where he should have been alert.
The picture shows him in an ugly
squat, all that Melville could coax
while dashing in and out of shot.
The collodion plate prepared,
I inserted it, ignored a pinch
of baited breath from the fist
of artists looking on then placed my cap

before the lens, removed it briefly
and let in the world:
at this there was some stifled laughter.
I do not despise the ingenious shutter
but my cap is my shutter. Sometimes
I use a book. With both I have succeeded.
And did so this time. That light can act
actinically in the twinkling of an eye
is no tax upon the cultivated mind;
for in this wink light has circled earth
twice at least and in this trice seen more
than man can ever see, blanched the picture's
subject with millions of fresh portions
that rebound to the lens and through it,
then nestle on the film. But could I speak
of this when afterwards they gathered
round to make inevitable comparisons?
Why did they chatter so when the photo
looked at them so frankly? Each splash
of light surging from the dark, each strand
of shadow surrounded by a ring of light
creates the illusion of looking at the one
who looks at it – even when no person
is present in the photograph.
I was lost in it, silenced, drowning
in pools of shadow that glanced
out at me like pupils from the white
of eyes; Lavery rescued me or rather
opportunely took centre stage:
as 'a young un', he'd 'retouched'
to McNair of Glasgow's *Herald*
drawn in a cloud or two – for skies
'just won't come out' – and rejuvenated
ageing relatives. 'For photographs so quickly
made', he said, 'you need very ripe collodion,
a well corrected lens, short focus
and a steady hand', at this he grasped
my hand and held it up, '– like M. Lestrange's! –
beneath the dark hood's tent.' His palm
was soft, soft as his brushes, as the feathers

I use to varnish the edges of my negatives.
He dropped it quickly, then turned
and fixing me without his usual smile:
'Sodium hyposulphate and acetic acid?
Ancient Egypt used this solution
to mummify their dead; its function
has not changed in several millennia:
thus, M. le Comte, you embalm
the living in baths and washes.
Like a sleuth you track the flux
of light and try to snare its vital spirit
in a print. You always fail for here
is shadow and more shadow,
a Grez of grey shades, a cave
in which the colour of the world is lost.
Yours is a necrophiliac art.' At this
there was a sharp intake of breath.
My own or from the others… I wasn't sure.
I bowed, retired back up the garden
and for a moment saw myself as they
must see me: an awkward human tripod half
cartwheeling,
the camera's hood flapping forward
like an elephant's trunk,
monstrous, most strange.

Midnight

Sleuth of the dandelion's seed,
of the sunbeam volatising
mica on the parapet, sleuth
of the night-time breeze,
its taste and touch,
of the current in the trees,
tree spit and froth, intricate
scum on the surface of the Loing,
sleuth of the chevroned wake
slipping from the tails
of swans, of the darkroom's tongue
where only the earth will speak.

'Sleuth': I looked it up: 'detective,
a sleuthhound on the track of crime',
a trapper, a sniffer out; of course;
but descending from the Norse word,
'sloth' which means both trail and trace.

Sleuth then of the world's
trace, the silver tracery
in the tree stump's bole
nested by spiders' webs;
trace of a world objectified
by light, of a person in the lit–up
world, opening lenses to it,
accompanying it.

'Sleuth'. He meant to hurt me.
And maybe Lavery too was something
of the sleuth: what was it in me
he sensed should be so hurt?
A strangeness; a nearness;
of art; of nature? It was when
he touched me I understood
his error, possibly his envy:

unlike painting, those traces
of the real in photographs
are not made by human hands
but by the real encounter of photons
reflected by the world's things
and the silvered surface of the film.

Lavery works with colour, pushes
little slabs and patches of it,
kneads it with scrabbling knuckles,
thumbs; it is wet and messy;
like the world but only like,
like, not traces of the world itself.

I stand before his paintings and look
at them. But he must step with his eyes
into the flat surface of my shady world
to recreate its depth and understand
the space that weaves between the objects
and the people shown there. He must be

a sleuth, like the maker of the photo,
retouch with his mind the images he sees.
He hurt me and I let him
because I wanted so much to smile
back beneath the dark hood
of my camera, focus on him,
straw-hatted man, model of mine,
centre him between my lenses.

Disruption

for John Fowler

My little nephew holds my hand; together
we stare up at the big picture, its rows
of Free Kirk ministers raked up towards
two skylights in a barn-like roof.
Pointing to a young man in a neckerchief
looking down on the assembly, he asks
'What's that one called?' I check my map
of all the holy folk: 'He's Willie Liston,
a local fisherman,' come to witness
the disruption of his church.

My nephew stretches up his hand, palm
open, then snaps it shut, as if he wants to open
up the tiny distant heads like windows in an advent
calendar. He's right. This box needs light:
washes, waves of it that Willie could drop
in nets upon the douce and sober company
who all await that Fisher of the guid elect.
His body blocks the aperture but if my nephew
prised these faces back upon their canvas hinges
he'd find them all in miniature, upended

on photographic slides the artist cribbed
their portraits from. Here, behind these windows
on the painting's past, the sun imprints
kirk bodies, lords and ladies, fishermen
improvising stillness with a liveliness
only the camera is true to: Willie Liston
'redds' his fishing line, a sturdy slouch
of crumpled clothes, his breeks and half
his face blanched to dough-like white.
He's ready in the changing weather, can't

stay for the exposure: five minutes
on the lens but twenty-three good years
before that picture of him boxed in against
the clouds is done. And so he leaves mid-
pose, bored by inertia, his features blurred
like the see-through cat that quit the shot
because the basket did not smell of fish.
The skylight fills up with a choppy sea,
a ghost boat steers from frame to frame
and there is Liston perching in the sunlit window

of a painting that inspired the one he's travelled from.
Beneath him now: a covered tennis court, French voices
bouncing off brick walls as revolutionaries
knock oaths of liberty, fraternity back and forth
across the mock-up of a lithe, impromptu parliament.
A gust of wind unfurls a curtain like a sail. It billows
through the dusty air carved by the slash of republican
salutes and Willie spies the features of a Patriot,
a Protestant, a President standing on a tailor's table.
The democratic crowd behind is sunk in too much light.

My little nephew looks up at Willie Liston sailing
on the pitched roof above the minute detail of his church.
The boy, the fisherman, seem almost spirited
away, caught in the half-light from two windows;
the bosun and his mate: out for a catch beyond
kirk and parliament, sounding the skylit deep
between two sketches of the world. My nephew
absent-mindedly strokes my hand then
turns and smiles at me: a grin without a cat.

Lob

A Platonic tennis match for two voices

LAVERY: A gleam from the crock of *écus* drives my brush, disperses light to every corner of the canvas;

LARTIGUE: canvas could not convey the fugitive chip and charge towards the hidden ball;

LAVERY: the hidden soul of tennis deposited in a little clinking velvet pouch at the origins of the game by fine Renaissance lords; it beats at the base of a wooden pole holding up the net;

LARTIGUE: the net's a vertical trampoline nothing and no one must touch, yet all align their posture, sweep, unimaginable leap only my camera can can upon its sly cross-hatch;

LAVERY: hatching slim lines to become the trunks of framing trees, I make shadow, contour, the three dimensions of the manicured hedge, its arch of mint; then a touch of blue, a memory of the River Loing: just the placid actuality of the Cart purling behind bland poplars I'd give French frisson to;

LARTIGUE: to and fro, fro and to… then click! Click, click!

LAVERY: Click away! My dowager black-gowned referee clicks her tongue: the ball is out; the lounger by the far right fence clicks with the girl opposite;

LARTIGUE: *that* click's the opposite of art: why just the light's suggestibility, the crumbs of story? *Tenez!* Here's a mix of limbs throwing up a lob as high as a Hail Mary;

LAVERY: and Mary is perhaps her name, a name spectators call out discreetly or with growing passion. And yet, you're right. I concede the point: this match won't gel, the figures are their figures corseted and crêped, booted in plus fours, a negligée of open shirts, flat caps, hints of bowlers, of breast-pocket handkerchiefs, bonnets and a rakish panama: the life-writing of hot clothes, cool wicker chairs, a tease of circumstantial detail. Yet each shred of narrative is worth a sitting in itself, each chap a portrait for which I'd make him dearly pay. That drink of water lounging by the fence could be Whistler and up ahead the story of his influence or a *fête champêtre*…

LARTIGUE: a *fête sportive*! Watteau did the aristocratic rural thing. Please spare us the bourgeois version! Look, here is Suzanne Lenglen, Nice, 1921: a little further up the centuries perhaps but – like the ball she's going to bat away in cricket fashion while still three feet above the ground – exactly in line with the horizontal slat of picket fence whose gang-plank dark is echoed in the Lenglen shadow leaping like a Matisse cut-out on the court. Head turbaned up against the sun, she feeds Egyptian gestures at the net, her face an ibis of precision, Nefertiti of the tournament, the imperium of movement stilled yet somehow still in motion.

LAVERY: But is it motion that truly moves and moves us as spectators of that motion? You're right! I can't catch it on my canvas. You've won the golden set, the slam! Master of the buggy whip, topspinning moonball, slice, spank and split-step, your photos serve the racquet's sweetspot to perfection;

LARTIGUE: perfection… of shot, of frame is not the effect I'm aiming at but a sense…

LAVERY: sense! Call it sensation! The volley of sensation and I have you in a break back!

LARTIGUE: Let's break it down then, as you wish: a sense of movement's violence;

LAVERY: violence of sensation more than violence of spectacle;

LARTIGUE: spectacle is cliché, the story of points won and lost;

LAVERY: but the body lost to pressure, weight, inertia, attraction, gravitation, even germination! If I could paint these bodies – forget about the light for once! – not as people, as members of the Cathcart tennis club or as white smudges figuring out movement but figures experiencing sensation, sustaining the sensation of being bodies in the world;

LARTIGUE: the world! Let's settle for the tennis court just now. We seem to have changed ends. Inadvertently. Your serve…

LAVERY: My serve then aims to finish with an ace, a *coup de grâce*!

LARTIGUE: *De grâce! Cher ami*, you're way beyond the tramlines! In the rough, the grass!

LAVERY: Yet grass is surely part of it, not part, no, but a beaten

Glasgow field that stretches from frame to frame dappled in every green, striated with pale mud, flecked with memory of lavender; a field that moves and curls, pushing its force up through the playing figures who in turn arch up, time stencilled through the changing textures, colours of their bodies, up to snatch the impossibly high lob and smash that force back down to earth so that I may help you feel not simply motion but movement in a place, a real place, athletic with life; a painting that would give you eyes all over, a canvas that invites me to take it from the easel and place it on the ground, work there, work in among the paint and mud, itself a fact of life, a future canvas where face and field will have the distances of the Sahara, a miniature Sahara placed at the feet of leaping players like a profane halo, its gold reflecting back their features, a coloured pressure balancing them, passing colours to each other like a yellow ball.

LARTIGUE: You've hit the ball boy on the head! You're just a hack, Lavery! 6-0, 6-0 I win: a double bagel, put that in your painting and smoke it!

In the rue Annette

This morning, Sir David Young Cameron
is trying to be Vermeer in the rue Annette;
it is not working. As usual he's taken
by the tilt and bevel of village houses.
But he can cope with that. Then he places
a seated figure just visible through an open
ground floor door: too distant to be enigmatic.
Upstairs, another seems to fuss with flowers,
and he's unsure if he should take her out or not.
The shop front is botched in chocolate brown,
the sun a slap of yellow; green shutters won't
fit and the word 'Epicerie' so solid it is as dull
as foreground shadows. He wants to stop
but a grey smudge crouched by the open door
will not allow it. What is his damn brush
trying to show him? And then he sees:
it is a tank, just big enough for an only
child to pedal. Quickly now he finishes it:
dates his painting *France 1919*.

A Backward Glance

i.m. Charles Rennie Mackintosh

There are plenty of ruined buildings in the world but no ruined stones.
                    Hugh MacDiarmid, *On a Raised Beach*

Seams, veins, flutes... and green for them,
green or an igneous yellow sparking
in the rock's black larynx. They pale
to a linen coloured path winding
its contour into schist. Bright rock!

I fail to fix you on my canvas.
Each morning, after breakfast, I travel
to my ear of stone down the wavering
trail of paint: tympanum, it shapes
the picture's echo, softening the see-

saw of my brush washing shell-like
on the surface. Each time I make a stroke
is like a backward glance
over ruined buildings. Och, what Tosh!
Margaret, who's away in London

seeing to her teeth would have a great hee-
haw at this: Bonjour Monsieur Orpheus!
Bathos aye hovers in the Port Vendres air.
I'll put it in the daily *chronacle* I send her,
then we'll chuckle eh? Margaret and her Toshy.

When I raise my head from this resistant rock,
the more distant landscape's leitmotifs
catch at the corners of my eyes: gulls,
tombstones, jib sails, each patch of white
lifts me towards the Canigou and that northern room

we worked and loved in. I see
two faces pouring over plans and lines,
disentangling to be roses, rooms
disclosing facets, snow-lit faces
like petals opening to morning.

My Margaret, named for a flower,
despite the art there was pea-soup,
dover sole and '*obergene*' in bacon fat
for lunch! Roast '*boeuf*', red cherries
and *Rock-e-ford*! The air was '*clair*'

and perfect. The '*Poupée*', '*Acola*'
and the '*Danielitto*' brought in
wood and gold to our sunlit harbour.
There are cobwebs on your chair.

At night the port wind builds
against the shutters of my heart:
brute slam of Tramontane,
dishevelled architect building
from the past's fast rock.

His shriek shakes, tears
from gulls behind the panes
or dies away – not quite, not quite –
a mosquito in the lull,
a fret of pain sawing at my ear.

On the harbour's starboard
a green light glints;
on its port, a red;
no letter though from Margaret:
silver beyond snow.

So then, begin again: picnic
on the ground bass, my '*cord du roy
écorché!*' Fumitory and rue hard by
entice the dead, my picture too I fear
as I ruin rock with paint.

Remember how I used to shape
the air we breathe, channel its currents
with posts and joists, float
the spars of human skeletons
high like kites then tether them
as temples to the gods of stone.

These wild cherries though
are divine! So grey, so ripe,
they dance on my tobacco tongue
ordering which portions of their taste
they take from life, from death.

Dance the cherry then! Like that other
Margaret, Margaret Morris who dances
in my memory just as the rock begins to dance:
each glitter of mica is a tiny meadow
in the stone, lit and capped by cloud,

and wings about her ankles
beat out the rhythm of the brush:
it winds down through stone,
tracing out a cage of stairs made
up of complex carpentry, loosening

its long hair to a white room
like a song; no, a white room
like the act of singing, a line
unfinished, whispering.

White room, black rock:
the private dream dies hard,
is hard, persistent as a cherry stone,
immured, declarative as those roses
made of lips and eyes;

eye-lidded schist whose texture
to the touch is that of wood,
a stony timberwork whose noggins
of bright rock refuse at last
all but the chaste succulence

of abstraction, my saviour:
divine geometry!

Between the Lines

Francis Cambell Boileau Cadell
'never indifferent to feminine charm'
did not marry, became a 'Bunty',
a playmate with a tartan face
who found aperitifs were 'necessary balm'
and made boys whisper at his approach:
'That's not a man, that's Mr Cadell!'

In shepherd trews, blue scarf,
yellow waistcoat or a kilt,
Uncle Bunty was a card;
in a white trenchcoat, collar
up, pipe and palette
clenched before a mirror,
he struck 'a gay and joyous note'.
A private in the trenches his uniform
was tailored privately.

The Somme was like Iona: a dreadful
dearth of baths: 'You either
stink or swim boom boom!'
Peploe sent a colour mag
to blot out mud and mud
yet Bunty wouldn't take commission
for anything but sketches
of the cocky Jacks and Tommies,
camerados in the lines.

The White Room, The White Teapot
Crème de Menthe, Carnations.
What explains his lust for white,
a creamy white, pursued across
the crunch of island beaches,
light's white: little bands
of spectra on the studio walls,
pink ladies, the odd pink man
who decorate the décor?

After the Great War everything was
flat. He took it at face value:
pleasure in a strand of sunlit carpet
linking joined but separate spaces,
the certain squareness of a room
saved from lumpenness
by an indefinable proportion.
He recalled the golden lining of a cape
pouring on a black and polished lake,

an orange blind with… something
blazing just behind. Once he painted
Able Seaman Vickers, twice
'a fine looking negro', often
his manservant Charles. And they were
full stops. Like the wink of ink
on Tommy's face, winks that spread
like ripples in Iona rock pools he never tried
to paint: going down and down
through emerald green

past the trench red of their sides.
And at the bottom there was death
again: flat and blank and white.

Mahlstick

Le Touquet beach flaps behind you.
Sand devils skitter along the car park walls.
The horizon is steel and rules out
a hundred lines of colour – fawn
through brown through cream –
as they descend, fray up
towards the streaks of pink
and a lozenge sun going up or down.

Small pyramids coast the water's edge.
There is a Rubens shaft of light on caves of space,
low skimming vintage planes, the sudden
gust of moule and frites cafés, all
the shut holiday flats, gays-in-the-dunes intrepid and alone,
polderisation, silting, salt meadows full of cockles and floating hides.

Razor shells crunch and glitter, signalling:
is/was is/was is/was

And here is the mahlstick,
snug on the canvas like the small, gnarled fist of a child.
Will it let you topple
as the brush hoves into view,
a spare rib floating free of the body?

Or will it let you
settle
lean into the world as it tips
away
to let you be
the spirit level of this place?

The Pink House, Cassis

Peploe painted this: pinks
mixed in with cream and a blue
pick out the compact oblong of a street sign
standing left of centre like the upright
hammer of a striking clock.

It is the epitome of equidistance.
A slash of yellow behind a picket fence
is the jazz age clarinet practising its plumb
line down the canvas from the open upstairs
windows. Angels live here. Or humans

with angels' wings. Step closer
to the painting. Place your thumbs
against the tiny grey-green shutters.
No. Don't close your eyes. Speak
as loudly as you wish. They

cannot hear or see you, attend
their only care: the stacks of canvases,
Palm Trees, Antibes, perhaps,
tablecloths like orange or olive deserts.
No wonder you fall silent

– as if an angel moved you like a picture
counting you among the fine still lives.
Stave off stasis. Take the tulips' touch,
finger their enquiring stems right
down to the root in teapots

where life grows riotously
from a side we can't quite see.
Peploe painted this: no petal,
no stem, no slight blue fissure
in any porcelain cup we ever saw.

The Place de L'Institut

i.m. Anne Redpath

When I pause (I always do) the *place*
is placid – no reason to pause – its blandness
a principle of the street that beelines
to the cute quay high and green
with *bouquinistes* above the gloomy river.
I sit down in the little square – its benches
for parked prams and dossers – glance
first at the fluted, broken fountain,
then at the large black grill – an echo
of portcullis – doubled by its shadow
that puts half a brass plaque in shade.
From here I make out two words only:
'Institut de'… What? Institute of what?
I know it's 'France' of course, but sun,
a slower current in the day, the need
to wring more from this banal angle of the city
prompts fantasy that doesn't come.
Why not? Because it is the Institute
of What? That sound: the upturned
blank space this *place* discreetly makes
of the universe we sit in eating lunch.
I could imagine but the blank walls,
high gate, the leonine knocker's
gold down-turned mouth precludes
all speculation. This is the domain
where academics are classed and paid
as civil servants. Imagine! Could I
paint this? Geometry would be
its only subject unless – somehow –
quintessence of blandness sugared
the picture suggesting an ironic
'thisness', a 'hereness' of the place.
This is the only canvas I have left.
War makes it scarce, me poor, doesn't
seem to touch the Institute, unmoved,
unmoving, even when Resistance fighters

are put up against its back and shot.
I close my eyes in the lukewarm evening sun:
like pottery growing bigger on a wheel
it whirls its ball towards my lids
and as I open them I see for one split second
a double-decker Edinburgh bus, red and silent,
cruise slowly round the square.
Why is it there? It is a 'what' in every tone
of voice the canvas may conceive
and if I paint these civic walls I'll sketch it
with equal gravity (more love) in chalk,
pink chalk upon the painting's back:
the raw, red hidden heart of the Place de l'Institut.

Eileen in a White Chair

after Anne Redpath

Eileen in a white chair
doesn't sit but hovers
closed lids like dark plump bees
feeding colour from her eyes.

Up now in the spreading
nectar Eileen isn't fixed in paint;
her salmon hands
might swim or pray
above her chequered dress.

Faint stencilled flowers
float up, lace or cup
her body; she stretches out
on leaf tip to pull their fabric close.

Eileen in a white chair
is an island in the lie
of pattern, a pebble
on the scumbled green
and the red paths of the world.

Helping with an Enquiry

i.m. Robert Colquhoun (1914–1962) and Robert MacBryde (1913–1966)

Excuse me, Sir, for interrup-
ting… but these ere cards… – 'monotypes' –
beg pardon, Sir, aint got the lingo
an your accent foxes,
these burnt papers anyhow,
these dubious if I may say so Sir,
images…

A clown's at – an 'arlequin' – av it
yer own way, Sir, a paper windmill,
a tin flute an a whistle blower – 'awker' –
Mr Col qwe houn you *are* the artiste after all…
Mr Mac Bryde I'm talkin to Mr Col qwe houn
thank you sir an I'll come to you in just a
mo…

Is this your landlady, Sir? What do you mean
'*A*' or '*The*'? Either she is your landlady
or she aint… If I can trace her she may be
called as a witness… 'to what, Sir, to what?!'
Well Sir I think you're best placed to answer that…
It's this one Sir troubles me most the one with the pig
init…

An the man… the personnage…
bending over its behind.
'A tufted hog' Sir? I dunno what you call em
up there in Bonny Scotlan but I know a pig
when I see im. You got a thing then. For animals I mean?
Item: an Essex carthorse, a circus goat, every bleedin breed
o cat…

that's ever scratched yer eyes out.
'Hieratic', Sir? Ow exactly do you spell that
now? 'Brack'? 'Pick who'? A Frenchman's wot? is finger?
A 'Glasgow kiss'? Don't you get funny with me, lad!
Stand by your portrait and don't move!
I'm commin to you now Mr MacBryde is that with an 'i' or a 'y'
by the
way…?

Excuse me for interrup
tin Sir. But this ere 'double portrait'
as you call it: *Two Women Sewing*…
Is that right Sir? Did the models ave names
by any chance? Were they twin sisters?
'Timber', 'cloth', 'machine': I can see all that sir; 'Naples yeller',
'Lenten purples';
Don't see…

an 'alter' Sir. Idden is it? 'Rapt celebrants'
as may be… Fingers dodging pricks
more like. You Sir? An… anim Sir?
(……………………………...............)
Ow do you explain the anged man
then in the cupboard behind your arses?
Maybe…
I should just call you both Robert?
Cuppla… Roberts………………..

Small Pleasures

This painting hangs in the mind's eye: a philosopher in a blue coat climbs up into a tree whose branches and leaves hang like a tattered map. He moves gingerly among the cities and small republics, his fingers inching over fluttering islands, the pollen of snow-capped peaks. Cherries stop him and he begins to pick them, throwing them down to two girls laughing on an ocean of grass. Rousseau – for it is he – is happy amid the cherry blossom and the cherries whose redness suggests the redness of lips. 'Why', he asks himself, 'are my lips not cherries?' So cherry lips rain down from the tree, lips laughing into laps held out to receive the gifts of juice and flesh. Lips and laps and cherries and hanging above the little scene the blue of the philosopher's coat whose folds and colour have the empyrean quality a painter sweated for, putting sky in clothes. This is cherry idyll, 'L'idylle des cerises'. But it is not a painting. It is an anecdote from Rousseau's *Confessions* and here and there, stray details, like traces of the brush's tip, make you pause and look or listen more carefully. For Mlle Galley and Mlle de Graffenried don't just catch the cherries, they throw the stones back up to Rousseau. Which means they eat them first, detach the soft flesh with their tongues and lips, spit out the stones then cast them back at the tree-hung philosopher. If you've eaten cherries you'll know just how much suck and careful tongue on teeth and palate is required to prise the stone from flesh. Do you swallow first or spit? It's a difficult job to do politely and then you wonder just what on earth the point would be of throwing moist stones back at a philosopher. His hands are full and his mouth is silent. Rousseau murmurs to himself, wrapped in his leafy fantasy. The moment when the cherry's flesh is consumed is not recorded, not depicted. In this rococo scene there is no munching maiden hunkered down beneath a tree and the cub-like aggression of the girls is only to be read between the lines. This silence is hot and lingers in the mind. Denis Diderot, Rousseau's one-time companion and lifelong enemy would probably have pocketed the stones, planted them later to make new cherry trees and told you everything you could ever want to know about a cherry. But when Rousseau climbs down from his tree, the stones are presumably still there in his deep dark pocket, now dry, knocking together like beads, fingered delicately in silence. Little cherry stones in a big blue pocket. Click. Click.

When the Scottish artist and poet, Ian Hamilton Finlay, revisits this scene in the twentieth century, 'cherry idyll' seems to be recast as cherry idol. The loss of a 'y', of an 'l', the addition of an 'o'. The slippage is minimalist but not minimal. Finlay homes in on the iconic qualities of the scene and abstracts them, like sucking the stone out of flesh. Or maybe not. Rousseau himself is banished, the young girls also. A bunch of red cherries are cast in white plaster of Paris and deposited upon a dish on top of a small, fluted neoclassical column. The title, *L'idylle des cerises*, wreathes around the foot. The column is placed in a charming grove of trees. Stephen Bann, one of Finlay's most astute critics, suggests that here we have a quintessence of pastoral, a still life that 'subsumes' Rousseau's 'dynamic rhetoric' and hints even at abstraction's future debt to the genre of still life. Finlay offers us an offertory of sorts, a fluted prayer to Nature.

Yet what strikes you most, perhaps, walking around Finlay's garden at Little Sparta is how much escapes or slips through the erudite mesh of commentary that is so vital a part of his art. Both the intellectual co-ordinates he deploys as part of the art-objects he creates and the critical work that accrues to it; a near silence that gathers around little stones. Bann doesn't comment on the fate of the cherry stones in the Rousseau anecdote, nor indeed does he take account of the deeply repressed nature of his 'rhetoric' as the passage develops. Shocked perhaps by the boldness of his 'lips as cherries' metaphor, Rousseau takes refuge in an insistence on the subsequent propriety of the day's events. 'Thus', he writes, 'we spent the day amusing ourselves at absolute liberty, but always with the utmost propriety.' Liberty, equality, fraternity, of course. But don't forget propriety. Ian Hamilton Finlay has not forgotten propriety either on his property of Little Sparta which is carefully mapped out and co-ordinated, the map that began this odd little piece having fallen, perhaps, from Rousseau's tree, its cantons scattering across the Scottish hillside. What happened to the stones in Rousseau's proper garden? In Finlay's, where there are so many, both natural and inscribed, you might be forgiven for wondering why the cherry stones didn't interest him more, more at any rate than the flesh of cherries reduced now in the pallid white of plaster. Perhaps that gesture of involuntary suppression – so Rousseauistic – is reversed, however, much later, at the time of Finlay's aborted commission to commemorate the Bicentenary of the French Revolution. If this had gone ahead, large stones – cherry stones swollen and distorted? – inscribed with sayings of the historian Michelet – cultural stepping stones and picnic sitting stones – would have separated a geometry of cherry trees. Rousseau's little cherry stones raining from his sky-blue coat, that pitter-patter, that flickering sound that skips through the garden like a breeze, like the nearly automatic shutter of a paparazzo's camera, or the infinitely repeated smack of Warhol-lips seeking lap upon lap, the sounds then of the idyll's repressed energy can just be heard, circulating against the artist's repeated attempts to plot or gesture deictically to the numinous, to hold it up as offering, as aura, to make an awe wood-lit, mind-lit, unique. Cherries as lips as butterflies, butterfly lips sipping at flowers but never stopping, still life only when dead and pinned in a cabinet of curiosities.

So much in Finlay's garden is moving and amusing. Reading *about* his art, his investment in tradition, in the great names, moments, movements of history, you can overlook how much less grandiose the actual experience of walking through his garden is. So many of the neoclassical ornaments that litter the paths are small and in their reduction, in this taste for the miniature which he carried with him from his adolescence, you can sense the real nostalgia for the gods who have fled, the gods and all their certainties, proprieties. And something of the admission of their regimes of violence is softened, surely, in this miniaturisation. The wit, the sense of humour dances forward. Even *L'idylle des cerises* is only waist-high in its modest grove of trees. And yet, perhaps, Finlay has not listened hard enough to this 'minor' mode. The most precious emotion may be the one that cannot be stilled, cannot be spoken, even – or perhaps espe-cially – aphoristically. It is the sound – again a 'sound' just heard within a garden breeze – made by the young revolutionary Saint-Just as he transforms himself in Finlay's mind into the figure of the god, Apollo: a boy becoming a god, not man and god or god in man, the sacramental creature of Finlay's inventive imagination but the young, blond haired boy running through a garden, the pitter patter of his feet like cherry stones on the ground, reflected momen-tarily in pools, in lochans, a boy among the leaves, lost in the aspen breeze before he is stilled by the hand of the sculptor, the axe man, and made to mean, even if that meaning is volatile and multiple. It is true that much of Finlay's art creates an imaginative and intellectual space in which the spectator can travel exhilaratingly back and forth between cultural co-ordinates but this dynamism is quite tightly controlled, corralled. As another eighteenth-century writer, Joseph Joubert, commented in a journal erroneously presented by that endearing authoritarian, Chateaubriand, as a book of maxims: 'Je finis trop: l'esprit du lecteur aime achever.' ('I conclude too often: the mind of the reader likes to finish off').

Look up at the philosopher picking his way about that map hung high in trees. There will always be a place, a branch on which he teeters and something falls or flies away without his entirely noticing. Once his name was Rousseau. A little later it was Tocqueville who confessed: 'There is something in the spirit of the French Revolution and its actions, which has yet to be explained. I sense where the unexplained object might be, but, in spite of all my efforts, I cannot lift the veil which hides it. I can feel it as if through some foreign body which prevents my really putting my finger on it, or seeing it.' For Tocqueville this revolution is a little queer, there is something that skites away. For Finlay this queerness is of a metaphysical nature but it could equally well be the repressed sexual energy that circulates in Rousseau's garden, the inconvenient, inappropriate scatter of stones the philosopher drops when his young friends throw them back to him. Roland Barthes' sensitive definition of 'eroticisation' comes to mind: 'Eroticisation is a product of the erotic: light, diffuse, mercurial; it circulates without ever becoming fixed: a multiple, mobile flirtatiousness links the subject to whatever passes, pretends to hold onto it, then lets go for something else...'

Of all the nineteenth-century artists though, it was poor, frustrated Ingres who felt this otherness, this queerness most acutely as he crouched before the blue robes of a Christ, enticing a 'jouissance' of colour from base matter. He became so angry at the distances apparently inhabited by the spiritual furled in that drapery wavering beneath his very nose; so obsessive in his need to prise open the folds of the spiritual for a deeply secular age. And something of Finlay's embattled nature has been heir to that struggle.

Perhaps it was just this current, breeze, call it what you will that Catherine Millet sensed on her visit – either actual or imagined – to Finlay's garden; this perhaps that she savoured even if she was unable to name it correctly so that when she lashed out at his attempts to still and contemplate and bring back – to her, oppressive – gods, humour and charity failed her. It is one of recent cultural history's choicer ironies that Finlay's arch-enemy, the journalist and curator, Catherine Millet, whose journal implied a fascistic streak in his art and campaigned successfully to have the bicentenary commission cancelled, has become the author of her own confessions: *Les Confessions de Catherine M.* I don't recall from her account whether Millet ever sought sexual fulfilment in a tree but it is clear from many other anecdotes that she has disported herself with much pleasurable athleticism. Rather than see Millet's wild 'impropriety' as the epitome of the Liberal not to say Libertine Terror that Finlay and the sculptor Alexander Stoddart have battled against, it might be more correct to define their respective cultural gestures as those of kissing cousins. In his search for transcendence, in order to escape the modern cult of self and personality, Finlay has appealed to the impersonality of tradition and it is clear from at least one passage of her memoirs that Catherine M. has sought her own escape from self in the reiterated pleasures of anonymous sex, her own search for transcendence in the momentary annihilation of orgasm.

Cherries are among life's small pleasures and it was on the site of the 'Hôtel des Menus Plaisirs' where the French revolutionaries first met and the Declaration of the Rights of Man was read that Finlay's forbidden garden of fruit trees was to stand. It was, perhaps, the suggestion of greater pleasures by means of smaller versions of them that have spurred the makers of dolls' houses to miniaturise some of Charles Rennie Mackintosh's tea-rooms and create a tiny version of the house the architect and his wife, Margaret MacDonald, might have lived in had they been more successful during their lifetimes and been able to enjoy the fruits of their labours. Unless the impulse is more complex than this: Finlay's early art began with the creation of 'little toys – things of no account in themselves, yet true to my inspiration, which was away from syntax toward the Pure'. And so the doll's house versions of Mackintosh may be seen as small icons, the perfection of their miniaturisation an unacknowledged attempt to restore to Mackintosh's art his own design on aura, his attempts to – literally – encapsulate the spiritual, the pure, now so acutely compromised in an era of mechanical reproduction. Such dolls' houses are further essays in the minor mode familiar in the work of

Finlay. They display – clearly another form of offertory – the ingenious articulation of architectural syntax, outside and inside simultaneously exposed – and at their heart the pure white rooms of Mackintosh's soul. They are small still lives, complete with their plywood figurines. If you stare at them quietly and for long enough they will provide you with the spiritual frisson that may not even be entirely available in the tourist-infested buildings themselves and certainly not from the plague of reproductions that litter cityscapes from here to Japan. Mackintosh's heroic struggle with stone offers, almost, an inversion of the cherry 'trope' as he places the chaste, succulent flesh of white and pink rooms within hard, fortified walls. Those who have said they could not imagine human beings managing to live in such aesthetic spaces are not entirely right. Those white bedrooms with their decorous alcoves, the inlays of pearl, the recesses of discreet opalescence are a clarion to love making. Not sex, no. But a slow ritualistic communion of bodies, the act itself haloed by the architectural and design-led co-ordination of a sacramental light. They offer a domestic reduction, a miniaturisation even, of the spiritual, making it manageable, proper, consumable (at least by the patrons, the owners of these expensive dwellings). Is it so fanciful to draw a parallel again between the tree climbing philosopher desperate to observe the proprieties, the social niceties and a later artist, Mackintosh this time, at home to guests? Fra Newberry's daughter recounts an anecdote that offers us a sight of the 'carefully chosen tea and cakes served with immense style among the white furniture of the drawing room'. The gods hover, as ever, just out of sight on the edges of this little supper. I doubt if cherries were offered as a chaser. Where would the guests have laid the cherry stones? When the flesh of a cherry is too ripe it can make you quite ill as Mackintosh discovered to his dismay in Port Vendres.

It is true though that Mackintosh's and Finlay's impulses, like those of Mondrian and Kandinsky and other great thirsters after aura are entirely human and entirely commonplace. It is visible at its most banal in the perennial turn to poetry in order to mark life's turning points or to help frame and define moments of great crisis. Then, poems are presented as icons, offered as prayers, for contemplative regard. Fixed on the experience of aura – the need to project or reflect it – they are removed from the ordinary energies of the reading process. This constant spiritualisation of poetry is always a simplification. Just as our understanding of the Ancient Greeks' take on painting as mimesis has been shown – by Stephen Bann – to be inadequate. He has argued that the art critics of the day did not expect simply an exact imitation by Zeuxis of a bunch of grapes but also an indication of their 'sensuous abundance', the product not so much of a creative 'vision' as of creative 'syntax' – that useful word Finlay eschewed – a creative dialectic between art and the world. So poems – even (especially?) poems about paintings – are always in excess of the given moment, they may be held up as a mirror to the scene of love, of crisis, but something always slides away on the periphery of vision. Perhaps the unique gift poems about art can offer us, precisely by virtue of being once removed from the 'original' subject of life, is an apprehension, however fleeting, of that 'excess', that 'abundance', a literal 'too much' that is the vital life of every poem. Savour those stones, moist and slippery: the philosopher tries to catch them but has his hands full of ripe cherries. Climb into the syntax, then, philosopher, poet, snake into the forks, the sudden impasses high in the tree: the Pure is always elsewhere and may be, in fact, simply an affect of the vertiginous manipulations of syntax as it responds to the body's mysterious energies. Poems happen while the frisson of meaning palpitates in the garden like a butterfly's wings, in that gap between the lyric and the critical which Finlay experienced as a creative abyss opening before him and spent his life trying to cross. But the true life of the poem is not – or not quite – in its construction of, or advance upon, contemplative stasis, however deeply desired that offering of spiritual sublime or quietude or the shuttle between them may be, but in the queer flicker, the pitter-patter of the cherry's stories as they fall and fly in the garden's sensuous breeze. Not still life but life, still.

Only for One

Dark Light: Alison Watt, Ingleby Gallery

Usually, when I have waited in dark rooms – silent except for laboured or anticipatory breathing and the drip, drip of an overhead pipe – it has been for the anonymous touch of human flesh. This dark room, however, enclosed within a 2.5 metre anodised aluminium cube offers art painted onto stainless steel walls, paintings barely lit by a dim, downward rim of light close to the ceiling, images of black convoluted, involuted folds that will only become visible after fifteen solid minutes of patience, of looking, of staring at and into the dark. As the gallery assistant ushers me into the cube, I murmur something pathetic and jocular about claustrophobia. I stand there semi-frantic, waiting for the zap of art, my fix, my fix, please my fix! But Watt has succeeded in slowing the spectator down. That at least. She has managed to reel me back into the nineteenth century when some of the Chardins, the Ingres, the Courbets, the Zurbaráns that lie behind this installation were painted and when – presumably – a different economy of looking, a different quality of patience was available. But to begin with, deprived of sight, I am singularly aware of my own body – as I was in those other, sexual rooms – of the slightly sulphurous smell of… plastic is it?… of something, of red floaters coasting the film of my eyes, of my own fidgetiness, my extraneousness, intrusiveness, fallibility. I cannot see what matters. Ever my curse. Then the deliberate attempt to suppress ego, to surrender to whatever might be making its way towards me in the dark. I am frightened I will see nothing. That it won't 'work' for me. What will this say about me, about my bloody eyesight? Me! Me!

The downbeat of the archangel's wing is preceded by a glimmering movement on the wall opposite. I think of fish first. Of a whale's rump drifting lazily into the terrible obscurity of an ocean. But the angelic wing is definitely there and clarifies itself in a way that is unsurprising and comforting. I am expecting epiphany and sex. That the religious comes first seems predictable and something for the developing clitoris in the bottom right hand corner to aspire to. The walls begin to flower with labia, shady hammocks – that long stretching sheen offering you in the end a place to lay your head –

the squash of crashed car tires, the wreck of James Dean. Yet these walls don't seem nearly as interested in becoming folds, in exploring the nature of folds, as Watt's previous white paintings done after Chardin. Each dark wall seems to float inexorably, although not always in the same direction or from the same angle, towards a black mouth or gap, an oblong fissure. These gaps seem to be the point of the walls. I will not lose myself in these folds, nor experience nearly the same degree of almost excruciating intimacy with lips and tucks discreetly offered and withheld, as I did with the white drapes. Paradoxically, this darkness does not lose me and I am not lost in it. Nor am I fearful before voids as some critics have instructed me to be. If anything there is a gentleness, an extreme peacefulness within this box, a desire perhaps to pacify. Do I want to be pacified? It is at this point that – to my dismay – the door opens, light floods in and a man steps in beside me.

Before the darkness engulfs us, we are able to exchange brief and slightly embarrassed salutations. But this does little to reduce the initial feeling of discomfort. The space is not large. My companion is slightly out of breath, is wet, breathes hard and drips occasionally onto the floor. I begin to perspire. We drip together. After a few minutes I think we both consciously make an effort to relax and resign ourselves to the fact that our epiphanies are likely to occur simultaneously, although my eyes have had more time to adjust to the dark than his and I am slightly ahead of him on this score. Of course I think of leaving but dismiss this quickly on the grounds that it might be interpreted as cowardice. My ego is definitely resurfacing. The man is relatively young and from the brief glimpse I have caught of him suspect that he might be attractive. I suppress other thoughts therefore, including images of scabrous tabloid headlines. This cube is *about* sex and the metaphysical but being metaphysical *in* it with another soul is definitely out of the question. I realise that my companion has displaced or somewhat reconfigured my experience of the art and conclude that this installation is only for one, for solitary pleasure indeed.

Again I become aware of my own body and its necessary accoutrements and understand that one of the reasons it has taken so long for me to become fully aware of the images before me is that the dim light from the ceiling has reflected off the frames of my glasses, minimally increasing the volume of light within the cube as a whole. The physics of this is probably wrong but it seems like it at the time. In fact, Watt's desire to invite the spectator into the heart of her paintings fails to take account of his – in this case – speccy nature. People who wear glasses normally see the world through a frame. Mostly they screen out this fact but this installation's contemporary ambition to bypass the traditional frame overlooks the habit humans have of carrying their frames with, about, within them. I try, then, to overlook my frames – brought once more to my attention – to overlook the young man – I'm sure he's young – beside me. For a moment we coast together. He is very still. So am I. We are definitely getting this. But we need more space, the space of a cathedral perhaps with all the stained glass windows blocked up: a quiet, black corner for votive lights, this tabernacle and its dark sublime. A canvas the size of a cathedral nave! And then the sheen of the archangel's wing would have freedom to swoop. Not this pinchbeck cube. This throw of a dice. And canvas, yes, not stainless steel! Watt's great skill is to evoke texture from and on texture and light shining upon it and in this black shiny box the light does not seem to catch, its detail less than visible. There is the *idea* of folds but not the swags themselves. I recall an interview with the artist in which she refers to several portraits in the London National Gallery that haunt her. A hooded, lugubrious St Francis by Zurbarán and Napoleon's Chief of Police, M. de Norvins, by Ingres. It is line, a shape she is looking for, pursued by, these men reduced to the minimalist dip and flourish of line and direction, emptied of content.

I look hard into the dark: which of these black swirls was the curls of M. de Norvins' deliciously glossy hair? I reproach the anecdotal impulse in me. But the gesture is fatal. Suddenly I see the police chief before me reclining – no, he doesn't recline, he's alert, tipped slightly forward in his chair – against a dramatically scarlet cloak that spreads around him like a lake of blood. He must have spilt plenty of it in his time. M. de Norvins, a youngish, very competent looking cavalier. Not to be messed with. The floor creaks as my companion shifts from one foot to another and then, of course, I imagine that this young man is himself a constable, off-duty, taking in a spot of art during his lunch hour. What other kind of person could conceivably devote his lunch hour to such a pursuit? It suits his métier exactly. He is a detective, a veritable Rebus no doubt, drawn by a weary, wary, minimally eager impulse to get to the heart of Watt's art. He is on her case. Is he on mine? M. de Norvins disappears but I have the strangest sensation that he has coalesced behind me in the shape of the young man. Oh my police chief! I have stood in dark corners with policemen before, or men who conducted themselves as such, and there is no doubting this firm presence. What swags pleat his living room? What curtains drape the intricacies of his existence? I turn in contrition towards my police chief, tempted to kneel on the dark confessional's floor. What do I wish to confess? What ecstasies of suffocation could these steel drapes perform? I sense a door behind a dark green velvet curtain, one that excludes drafts and whispers and then on the wall before me the shadows of a figure – de Sadian – glide with slight, mocking laughter into the gloom. The door opens and we stand together for a moment, my police chief and I, framed and dazzled in sunlight, an archangel with his novice on the threshold of a photograph. Our eyes blaze in consort, the gaps of our mouths are golden, our flesh black as carbon. There is a sigh but it comes neither from M. de Norvins nor myself. I take this as a cue to exit and do so.

I hang surreptitiously around outside the cube, running my fingers over its cold, sleek surface, determined to get a better look at my companion when he leaves. How he must be savouring my absence! But after a while I realise no one will emerge, no bright and cheery student clad in his red anorak will step forth. Nor will I look after his departing figure with certain, lugubrious relish. For my pleasure has been solitary. I have had M. de Norvins all to myself. And he is still in there. Still. As I buy another small catalogue of Watt's white paintings, the gallery assistant enquires witheringly after my claustrophobia then hands me some small change.

Thyrsus

...around this baton, in capricious meanderings, stems and flowers twine and wanton.
Baudelaire, 'The Thyrsus', *Little Prose Poems*

'*I am Muriel Gray. I'm a writer and broadcaster.*' A child has pressed an interpretation panel on a screen and Muriel leaps into life, her voice loud down the gloomy gallery. You bob between display cases and catch odd words, a phrase: '*his hand round this lovely gnarly stick*'. What stick? You peer through glass at tartan mannequins, a broach of hare foot, Charlie's, Flora's, '*telling us a bigger story that tells us everything, not just about being Scottish but about the world*'. Muriel unwinds the narrative and you catch a glimpse of her hands clawing air, '*he actually held that, his hand actually went round it*' and then you see the stick itself, Robert Louis Stevenson's walking stick right next to the first Scottish golf club. There is no visible means of suspension and like a tape worm dried from the nation's bowels it floats through the viscous air. '*The man that wrote Kidnapped, Treasure Island and it's here.*' It's here, a simple curve of wizened wood right amid ships of the dawn. '*Can you imagine the excitement?*' Knotty carbuncles stand out like ancient button mushrooms from the surface and you can just make out a small heraldic shield. What can it say? Outside, the day star sparkles like a diamond but in here, here at this '*case in point*' deep among the interpretations '*I am Muriel*'. Did he cut this stick himself from Fontainebleau Forest, tramping from Barbizon to Grez? Did the little wild boar nuzzle at its tip? '*Can you imagine the excitement?!*' Or did it switch a donkey's back, act 'mahlstick' to cousin Bob's painting of French peasants à la Millet? This virtual world tips tipsily at its pointed tip. Lean in, lean in: '*I'm a writer and broadcaster*' and try now for the land breeze that smelt strong of wild lime and vanilla; the wood of the stick exhales it, the memory of sap, of Samoa, the indifferent beach, the gutter, driftwood people it flicked away in ink and spittle. '*This is not the classic Victorian ebony and silver cane. No spats here!*' if you please. Look at the dark gouges in the wood. Look closer at the miniature caverns which echo to the cries of shipwrecked sailors. '*You can't get better than that!*' Twist your gnarly hand in a squall of frenzied tapping. Take the porridge-stick, the stick that would not burn, the stick with which the deed was done, its evil pewter knob that clicks on stones and skulls. '*He actually held that.*' A great rooty sweetness of bogs is in the air, '*I am Muriel*' and his hand is round this lovely excitement, this bigger story of gentle little mutinies, sad little gaieties, this stick that, as it were, withered in the growing. Yes, '*I am Muriel*', menseful, a design in snow and ink, piercing the joint of fact, rosy with much port. Keep me, Mr Weir!

In the Beinecke Library at Yale there is a letter from Sidney Colvin which states that Robert Louis Stevenson never owned a walking stick.

5/cinq

after Douglas Gordon

Spit sweat number cinq! Head, pass, trot, walk... Zinédine! 'Hey!'
Twirl. Twist. Points to a space and enters it, tackles, gets clapped.
Almost bow legged. Zidane. Zidane. Nothing. Nothing. A blur.
Blur! 16 7 11 6 5 5 5 5: the strapline phones you, tells you it's *Ulti-
mate Diesel*, *Ultimate Gasoline*. His head, head lit by a silence and a
speed he borrows from the small white ball we hardly see. Framed
by the absent ball. Where will the little ball come from? Blocks,
passes, sweats, drips. An earring of sweat. He courts the soft prison
of the net. Horns, drums, chants dowsed to the static of commen-
tary. Horns like a distant traffic jam. Flurry of legs, *rafale* of grunts.
Head! He peers into space like an old woman. Toreador, sheepdog
head, the sweat glistens like wet paint. A rather austere accountant,
his feet strapped like a ballet dancer, Zidane does the wader mince.
Zinédine Zidane! The stillness is upset and counts. Time enters the
picture. Naples yellow from Velasquez passes white stockinged legs
in an abstract shot. *Kellogg's Frosties*. Parabolas. Drums. Catcalls. The
kissable mouth of Vitruvian man half open, open... for as long as it
lasts, as long as it takes. Being panther-like, run backwards to your
work, its intensity, its fluidity and stasis, the entering and leaving
both, dark epic, leap and enter the pixels of *le carré vert*. 5! Cinq!

Self-Portrait of the Artist as a Barbie Doll

Doll, I stand, maybe sit, half-
turned towards you – mirror
mirror framed in gilt – clock
you with little sidelong
glances then scurry back
to home and work in paint.

What is it turns you on
the most about me, Doll?
Ringlets beneath a thumb-
sized hat? Pink inkles
at my ankles, the buik
of maxims in my whittled fist?

Clear the foreground clutter Doll:
the *petits pains*, the *petit point*
the cherries on a dirty platter;
surely that cypress-laden meadow
tucked in behind your pint-sized
shoulders gives you the crumbs

of story you need to map
the ways of being other men
and women. Doll, peek out
from the shadow box
of your doll's house windows,
quit the hood, the doorless cube.

Sleuth! The poor world
lies there behind you,
stranded in its loch of paint.
Look up, look out!
The gulls and jibsails
white patches of almost everything

are passing, passing;
while the mirror fills with a face
so thin you could make coin from it.
You swim towards me from the pond
of night and in the artificial light
– Horror! Horror! – here is my most sweet

seraphic toy: an index finger
seemingly detached by shadow
pointing squarely at my heart.

Finger of a Frenchman

Finger of a Frenchman

for Jonathan Sawday

Did the finger first reach into
or out of candle flame? Perhaps it wavered
like the old man I have become.
Or was it supple, the finger of a brown hand,
firm with travelling veins,
neat nails, corrected cuticles forming
half moons below a tip of pearl?

I weigh the odds, sip a second
glass of port, hunch up my gouty
body in its woollens;
so the flame flickers on the past's
inventory: this catalogue of my cabinet
of curiosities. *Item*: one old cleric
wintering in his lists and marginalia,
knitting his body out of dubious collectables.

And yet I would in no measure be
dislodged: not for warmth, not
for the slightest friction of that stroking
finger licking its slender
flame about my table.
At Bifrons, when I was young,
my father's wealth was measured
in the candelabra he lit and hung
from ceilings high as naves:

I swam in rooms that glimmered like aquaria,
a minnow, then a goldfish, bumping
the small 'o' of my mouth against
the pier glass mirrors and steaming
them so I could draw the fish I was:
and then my mother told me I had drawn
the Christ, that I would grow
to be a fisherman of men like Him.

I give Him praise and toast Him
– with another glass of port.
Holding it against the writing flame
the past does not seem as rosy
as the future did to Master Bargrave
sheltered from his family's flaws,
ambitious farmers to the King.
Don't think on it just now; a lifetime
of such thought has brought me
to this modest pass:
Canon of Canterbury Cathedral;
what could have been
is past.

Item: *a little key, dug out of the Temple
of the Moon.* Will it then unlock
the meaning of this severed finger
that inscribes its partial scripture
on the wall? For it is not the shadow
candle flame alone. I know it, cannot
say it, write it, because of all the other
words and images that well up
trying to drown its voice. Once

I pressed my knobbly boyhood knees
against the goldfish pond in uncle's courtyard:
'Do not go home today,' I had been told,
'cousins wait; play with the Comets and Commons
that graze among the reeds.' So I stroked
the brackish liquid under the udder-shapes
of clouds; all thickened in a leaden summer heat.
Time moved like a carp in water
as I suppressed and clenched
the cry of 'oh my father!' forcing my hand
to move as slowly, slowly as the smoke
that curled up from the known, unseen source.

Months before I'd lost myself in names
and colours: the playful schooling Black Moors,
the midnight blue of Lionheads
with calico and lemon snouts, the omnivorous
Bubble Eyes, Shubunkins, Orandas; on my uncle's,
then my father's knee, I told them all like beads.
Now, just one common goldfish glowered
in the deep like a struck medallion and although
I would have kept him down, far down,
slowly he surfaced to nudge my hand
and in the chain mail of his tiny scales
I saw the burnt umber of reflected clouds
coloured by the cull of cattle, the smouldering
dispossession of our house just five miles down
the childish Kentish lanes.

Raised to a Fellowship at Cambridge
despite the times, I looked upon the heads –
domed, ruffed and hatted –
of bright young men and failed to notice
some of them were Round: one
placed upon my desk a Venetian
stiletto, steel tip towards my chest;
pocked with deep thin slits
no balm or salve would reach
its inward and unequal scars.

I marvelled at the curious thing
and at the boy belonging to it,
demitted office, went abroad.
Still I had no luck with younger
men: beholden to yet governing
aristocratic offspring on five
Grand Tours unbearably extended
to fit the Farmer's tenure of the crown.

Then it was temples, aqueducts,
cirques, naumachias and heathen medals
dug from endless ruins. I went
to goldmines in a wheelbarrow
with the Duke of York, walked
streets of catacombs and left
my tears in bottles by storied
corpses immured in *thecae*.

Once I heard the famous
Finch and Baines had called
– medics and diplomats
en route for the Porte;
they left respects in pen-
tameters that wrapped themselves
about the endings of their
never-ending lines. Still:
I kiss their phantom hands.

At length I took the title of 'collector'
just to stem sightseeing's boredom:
so I began: – *imprimis* –
with an infant Romulus in brass,
a handsome dusty *busto*,
a Leda with her swan.
I bartered for the knuckles
of an ancient bone of mutton,
a pretty little padlock
and a key of gilt.

My most intense and compromised
delight: this mummified
finger of a Frenchman,
got at Toulouse from a nun
and bought in lieu of a small child's body
– part for whole, alas, but I was outward bound.
I keep it in the deepest recess
of my cabinet yet it twitches
when this other disembodied finger writes upon my wall.

I wonder if it's an optic trick…
of God who laughs at my pretension.
I pull the stool up and try to stare the tireless digit
down: how is it I can see the finger
clearly but can't make out the script?
I stretch out my own and touch it:

nothing happens; I touch the wall,
the finger does not flinch, writes
on and yet that crook of bone
is known: surely it bent to beckon me
at Rome? The papable finger
of a princely priest I annotated
in the margins of a book presenting
Portraits of the Cardinals. (It passed
the time.) Is it Costaguti's index?
The 'Golden Cardinal' whose dignity
cost him three times more than it is worth?

No; the way it hooks the quill
reminds me of Capponi
who strung up two gentlemen
caught with pistols in their pockets.
Only this. I hired a chamber
to see the execution:
clubbed, flayed, quartered,
heads, livers, lungs hanging
from their windpipes, shaved
privities, all hung from poles.

'Ma questa e la giustizia de preti' –
But this is priests' justice! railed
the medical dissectors, wringing
hands beneath the gibbet
at so much wasted flesh.
And does this finger now
dissect my life, these words
within the margins of this wall
a commentary I cannot read
because the subject's dead?

Or good as. I pull the stool up
closer still: it is the finger
of every cardinal dreaming
the blossom of his popedom,
entering conclaves Pope,
exiting as Cardinal again,
the rapacious, disappointed
finger of every *illustrissimo*
I carried letters to, seeking
protection, licence to carry
books and curiosities
for my cabinet. My cabinet…

The finger writes from shadow
into sunlight: I see the carpenter
I hired to make it caught incising
his initials on a hidden panel
within a secret drawer.
I let it pass. He was childless too.

John Evelyn scoffed at it, cited
the *wunderkamer* of his travels,
cabinets of damascened iron,
'niello', gold and silver, 'tesserae',
'intarsia' of assorted woods
and within: the twelve apostles
of incomparable amber.
Pretentious man! He called
my 'box' a coffin and quipped
that I should sleep in it like Donne.
I am no Poet, eschew veneer and marquetry.
Dovetails are for bishops; joinery for canons:
tenon and mortice fit my cabinet out and sometimes

when I stare at its plain hardwood screens
it seems capable of shaping
all my dreams upon its wooden skin,
pales to a translucent sheen
and there within, each curious
object – mere replicas perhaps –
glows in a sap-lit light like organs
in a body, their sense and purpose
open to the touch of sight.

And once or twice this box
of dreams dreamt me,
shot out its arms and legs
as arches, pillars, made me
walk within its cabinets:
the small green boy of Bifrons,
a father's curiosity, lost
among collectibles destined
to be pawned.

I see him still, a tiny figure
in a *studiolo* or enclosed
garden boxed by box hedge:
Item: *a maimed Mercury,*
with one arm and one legg;
dugg out of his temple; ancient.
And my father pointing
at the little message of his son,
still as a statue that might
move and heal if touched.

I lay the figurine flat
upon the fruitwood bier
and watch the god of medicine
– *item: an Aesculapius in bronze* –
prepare my rags for their anatomy:
supine, I watch his royal fingers
curl out to mine which curl
back mechanically and are not touched or touch

and when I reach within
the little death of sleep
to stroke his hand I clutch
– *item*: the shrivelled finger of my Frenchman.

Once, on a stairwell in a foreign city,
that finger grew a hand – soft palm, hard
fist – became an arm that pressed me
close, a chest that opened up a whole
man to me, who placed an ear above
my heart and listened for its responsive
beat. And yet it fluttered like trembling
fingers that grasped but could not
clasp; fingers that drummed on hollowness,
able at hinges, springs, the secret coils
of cabinets but whose pulse sounded
like a muffled echo sunk in wood.

Once, at Paris, before a tailor's shop
in Montaigne Street, I stood and gazed
through Monday rain, seeking a light,
a figure closing up, moving towards
a forbidden tryst we'd only half-
arranged. Only the rain moved in,
closer, fiercer and words I sent out
with shallow breath, or the odd
intake, stepped into falling drops
that beat their salt upon my face.

Once, at an auction near the Forum,
I saw you vying with friends:
you bid laughingly for two *Priapisms*
in brass, modern from ancient,
and I mutter on this deity's absurdity.
But then you buy a small Salerno ring,
a posy inscribed within its inner band
of words spoken by the Virgin to Aquinas.
Did you glance towards me then
from the corner of your eye
as you gave your friend that ring?

Bene scripsisti de Me, Thoma
the posy rounds on me.

On maps some mountains
are like bruises. I climbed
the bruise of Vesuvius,
three times to the puckered rim
and looked out to England,
England. I felt a fool:
Ischia's red diamond
moved liquidly out of focus.

Oh, my finger of a Frenchman!
   The corn was Orient –
You cut a swathe through crowds
   Immortal Wheat
stalks and children who were
   moving jewels
bowed and I seemed to stand
   from Everlasting to Everlasting;
in the street – I can name it! Name it! –
   The Dust and Stones
saw me, saw you,
   Green Trees Ravished me
and I tried to remember, try to remember
   yong Men Glittering and Sparkling Angels,
words you spoke to me
   strange Seraphick Pieces of Life and Beauty
as you passed me by.

The City seemed to stand in Eden.
The streets were mine.
I knew no Churlish Properties.
Nor bounds. Nor Divisions.
So that with much adoe
I was corrupted.

I conjure that man from you again.
I am ready now. John Bargrave
at seventy is ready now: the beat is
pristine, manly, virginal
and still the finger writes
upon the wall opposite my bed.
It may not stop just yet.

So I recompact the sweet body
of that Frenchman out of a shrivelled
finger that tap, tap, taps my cabinet's partitions.
'For distributions are great things in Art.'
And yet he taps: the tiny priests' holes
slide back to show leather bags
containing desiccated nails
which he puts on with ceremony
then knocks again on drawers
that swell to doors and open
on a very theatre where his wholeness
lies unwoven, awaiting weaving,
the knitting up of flesh that lies
beyond all partial words.

Now the curiosities cohere
and through the frail prism of my box,
the slight, deft carpentry
of its frames disclose him,
small, complete, an other
man in the other world of life,
dressing in his cabinet,
choosing which of the Bifron
faces he will wear about
his resurrected house.

Suppose a River.
Suppose a Drop of Water.
Suppose an Apple.
Suppose a Sand.
Suppose an Ear of Corn
   – that corn –

– that day –
Suppose an Herb

their infinite excellencies

Suppose

What a World would this be

★

But still there is an ache
within my room:
there is this uncanny
reversal: the limb missing
its body, the far from phantom
pain. Suddenly I understand:
my soul nests on its cuticle,
balancing upon its tip,
a tiny tennis ball
that has bounded back
and forth across the courts
of Europe. It is frayed.
The cork is showing.

More soberly then I review
my modest doll's house collection:
mostly rubble, butts of obelisk,
small cinders, ashes, flakes of life's
shuffle; the odd rich one
like this very artificial anatomy of a human eye
with all its films by way of turnery
in ivory and horn: I turn

its optic nerve upon
the neighbouring curiosities:
it sees a hundred faces
carved upon a cherry stone,
each one with a look
of cardinal or churchman

stacked above pews
or endless galleries, seeking
a window in this airless cabinet.

It sees the nameless figurines
stalk empty corridors between
the drawers, stick heads into draped
black boxes for a sunbeam
in the shadows, for fragments
of a young man pointing to an apple
and find instead a tiny watch
placed in the jewel of a finger ring
which pricks at every striking hour.

My 'box', my marginalia...
And yet they register – just –
(just dear God, but just enough)
that I am here, here on this patch
of Canterbury earth, lodging
precariously above crypts
and tombs, can see in this candle
the brightest light my life
has ever seen, and that I,
John Bargrave am seen
in it and have been seen.
(Nothing can diminish this.)

The finger's script now shines
in sunlight: what does it say?
mene, mene, tekel, upharsin,
'numbered, numbered, weighed
and divided'.

After Words after Art

for Cheryl Follon

moy qui fais profession des choses muettes
Nicholas Poussin

'You merit Fatwa!' The letter began tastelessly enough but the cold enumeration of my deficiencies that followed did not stir me, initially, to feelings of justified outrage. Indeed it merely confirmed a sense of despondency that had crept ever closer as I approached the end of my sequence of poems about paintings and prepared to write the critical preface I had promised patrons and benefactors. Some dyspeptic poetry bodie – a disquietingly numerous breed – had got wind of my project and the stalker now wrote to me in a blatantly malicious attempt to put me off my stride. Little did they know, however, that I had been tottering for some considerable time and that their letter was the epistolary equivalent of a *coup de grâce*. The fact that it was a letter I had received rather than the thin gruel of email or the scattered bird shite of SMS merely reinforced my growing conviction that I was engaged in a deeply antiquarian endeavour of interest only to… well, antiquaries. This letter-writing antiquary was sufficiently self conscious to recognise the grizzled character of his own protest but rude enough to blame me also for dragging him down to my own level: among his accusations was that of my utter redundancy, my backward-looking, nostalgic necrophilia as I rooted among the second rate canvases of the past.

Furthermore, the author of this missive had not typed his message. It was written upon three crisp new sheets of Basildon Bond. The hand was bold – everything about it was bold – but at first I was unable to make out the signature. This unexpected contrast gave me pause: a large hand accompanied by a tiny name. Was the ultimate moment of confrontation to be one of detumescence? Had the infernal scribbler lost his bottle at the last moment hoping that the inscrutability of his signature might prevent me from giving wrathful chase? Or, more intriguing still, did the sudden miniaturisation that overtook him signify an implicit doubt as to the merits of his argument? I searched in my bureau for my late grandmother's magnifying glass and looked again. Perhaps I had simply mistaken the neat for the tiny… The shock was instantaneous. I staggered back and sat down hard on my faux Louis XV. This was nothing other than monstrous. I felt like a character in a fiction by Poe unjustly pursued by a fury of his own obscure making; for here surging beneath the bevelled glass was the name of my police chief, M. de Norvins. *Mon lecteur, mon frère!* We have met him before! This was uncanny because to my certain knowledge the prose-poem that features this well-dressed thug appears in this collection for the first time. How could my interlocutor possibly have intuited the significance his name would have for me? I suspected occult foul play and crushed the offending letter with a single manly gesture.[1]

I returned to my cup of decaffeinated Nescafé and prepared to brood. This was too bad really! To be so close to finishing and then to have this brutal wad of prose thrust under one's nose. I began to fantasise: in my original application to the Arts and Humanities Research Council for funding to support my endeavour I had been assigned a 'case officer'. Was it him? Was this 'M. de Norvins'? Did this poor, underpaid invidual have nothing better to do with his time than ghost my collection of poems, becoming so involved in the devious intricacies of its 'case for support' that he was able to intuit the images and protagonists of the poems themselves? Was the AHRC endowed with some ghastly form of osmosis that enabled it – spookily – to anticipate the outcomes of investments that did not quite come up to scratch and to subvert them in this mole-like manner, enabling the august institution to reclaim at some future date its initially misguided award? Or was M. de Norvins a scion of that other body, the Scottish Arts Council, who had also given its generous support to the folly I was engaged upon? I went to the window of my sitting room and gazed out across the city. He was out there, somewhere, M. de Norvins, in the wynds and vennels of Glasgow, perhaps even now penning a second attack upon my ekphrastic art.

The word stuck in my craw: 'ekphrastic'. This was the kind of term – which for now we may translate simply as poetry about visual art – I was duty bound to reflect upon in the critical preface I had so

---

1   In fact, the author is mistaken. This prose poem appeared for the first time in an issue of a little magazine called *PS* edited by the esteemed poet Richard Price, some time before the publication of this collection. (Ed.)

rashly promised my patrons, one of whom even now appeared to be 'on my case'. What on earth had possessed me? Who ever heard of a poet attaching a critical preface to his own slim volume of poems? The hubris, the sheer impossibility of the project astounded me. The lure of lucre of course. At the time I would have promised anything – Faust-like – to get my paws on the money that would buy me the time necessary to write what I really needed to write. I had no idea at all what that was, of course; no poet ever does, really. But I persuaded myself that the poems about art could be written gaily in the margins of that other secret poetic endeavour: the one no one would ever fund me to write because it could only exist at the moment of writing. And now, I mused bitterly, Mephistopholes or Shylock has come to claim his pound of flesh.

I turned back to the crumpled letter and began to smooth out its creases. I stared at it balefully for a few minutes sucking disconsolately at my coffee. And yet – if one put one's pride on the back burner for a moment – there was something touchingly naïve in its amateur sturdiness. Supposing, I mused, supposing I were to take it even more seriously and pretend that it was entirely fictitious, that M. de Norvins was not a real, living person but a Socrates intent on initiating a kind of platonic dialogue in which the pros and cons of my poetic sequence might be debated...; such a form – neither critical treatise, nor lyric meditation or epistolary rejoinder but...well, such a form might permit me to fulfill my obligations and confront what I was beginning to recognise as a fundamental scepticism towards the merits of exegetical prose.

I forced myself to re-read the string of insults which the author had listed thus:

- Have you not read – dolt – Gotthold Ephraim Lessing's *Laokoon: An Essay on the Limits of Painting and Poetry* (1766)? Poetry is a time-bound art; painting inscribes space.
- You fiddle in the margins of the margins: Rome burns! Sunk in Plato's cave, you provide the imitation of an imitation.
- Why focus on this Franco-Scottish theme at a time when nationalism – in all thinking circles – has such a dubious name?
- The intrusion of one art form on another inevitably raises the issue of what art is and thus we get yet more poems about poetry.

Masturbation, Sir! Masturbation!
- Nobody paints these days! Concept and installation are all.

My first instinct was to register the slight disjunction between the appeal to a text dating back nearly 250 years and an evidently superficial appreciation of the trends of contemporary art. Each point contained a measure of truthfulness, some more than others. But, I wondered, could Lessing not be made to hold his peace in the face of the wonderful writers – Mallarmé, Joyce, Proust and Pound among them – who had discovered means of representing and suggesting spatial qualities in language? And yet, I admitted uneasily, few of the poems in my collection proceeded in such overtly modernist ways. Considering my antagonist's second point, I reflected that the initial impetus for my collection had come from a dissatisfaction with my practice as a poet: I found previous collections needlessly solipsistic. I had wished to turn away from the self and its obsessions and look out into the world. That my gaze had been able to settle only upon art objects in galleries and museums was further proof, perhaps, of a fundamental distance separating me from the living and the actual. On the other hand, the pull I felt towards many of the paintings I have evoked might be construed as a healthy curiosity about what visual art may accomplish, an implicit admission that the limits and expanded possibilities of lyric poetry – of art itself – are indeed brought into intense focus in this raid upon the silence and stasis of other art forms. The attack on the 'nationalistic' flavour of the collection was of little importance. The theme had been conceived as little more than a convenient angle from which to approach ekphrasis and was a matter of taste more than anything. More moving was the thought that poems about paintings make visible and, in a sense, audible, the usually silent act of reading as the reader of the poem inevitably reproduces the reading processes of the writer who contemplates and interprets a visual text. As for M. de Norvins' fourth point: this was the weakest of all and I took some crusty pleasure in imagining the length of the cul-de-sac that swore by the conceptual alone.

Then, however, I presumed that he said something interesting. I stress that the following exhortation was not in the actual letter I received from M. de Norvins. But at this point my subconscious prompted me to invent an admonition that intensified the sense of unease that had accompanied all my squirming and reasonings, faithfully reproduced above, intensified it to a point at which I was forced to hunt through my shelves for the book he might have mentioned in the final paragraph of his letter. 'Read T.J. Clark's *The Sight of Death: An Experiment in Art Writing*. It will stop you writing your bloody ekphrasitc poems for good. This will be an immense relief to you and a deliverance for us.'

I sat bolt upright in bed for by now I had retired there with my quill and candle. I knew this book! I had read this book quite early on as I prepared my applications to my patrons. Could it be that M. de Norvins had – quite unbeknown to himself – dropped a vital clue to the nature and structure of the very book of poems he was complaining about? He was not a Chief of Police for nothing! Could this wonderful book – I agreed entirely with my adversary on this point – actually be the unconscious well from which *Finger of a Frenchman* had emerged? Far from shutting me up, as my little policeman possibly imagined, it had provided me with a set of implicit, unacknowledged, deliberately forgotten compass points from which much of the poetry in my collection had taken its orientation. I could see the cover clearly in my mind's eye. The fragment of a face from a painting by Poussin entitled *Landscape with a Man killed by a Snake*, a face haunted by the sight of death about to turn away in its flight towards life. And Clark's book was focused solely on this one painting and a comparison of it with another by Poussin called *Landscape with a Calm*. For a while they had hung on opposite walls of the Getty Museum in Los Angeles and each day the art historian had returned to look at the paintings and record his impressions of them on a day-to-day basis. What was it about this strange book that had so captured my enthusiasm?

Well, for a start, this is a book with poems in it, poems about art. It is a curious hybrid that does not seek to contextualise Poussin's pictures using the type of discourse typical of an art historian. Indeed, it is written in the teeth of this type of practice and underpinned by a strong belief that looking at Poussin, far from being a nostalgic, reactionary activity, offers a form of resistance to what Clark calls 'the present regime of the image' where technology seems to have permitted the 'threshold' separating verbal and visual worlds to be crossed to the detriment of both. The stress here is on the word 'seems'. Clark is clear that this is itself a 'story' in which he does not believe. Instead, Clark offers us a patient, painstaking account of a process, the process of looking again and again at the same two canvases with the conviction that images do not 'happen all at once' as many people assume. He returns to the gallery day after day, not in the hope that he will be able to offer an explanation of these paintings, of how representative they are of the artist's work, for example, or how they relate to other art works of the seventeenth century, but in the hope that by a humble process of description he will be able to suggest – paradoxically – what it is about Poussin's art that lies beyond language, that is not para-phrasable. So the figure of Gotthold Lessing and the Laocoon reappears but with a modern slant: 'I believe the distance of visual imagery from verbal discourse', he writes, 'is the most precious thing about it. It represents one possibility of resistance in a world saturated by slogans, labels, sales pitches, little marketable meaning-motifs.' Only a description, a simulacrum almost, of the material effects and practices evident on the paintings' surfaces can hope to avoid betraying their essential 'silence'. The word 'paradox' needs to be repeated here: Clark has to admit that what he is doing is 'looking generated out of writing'; discourse, criticism, interpreta-tion – call it what you will – hover menacingly, enticingly at the edges of every page. What are also present, of course, are the recog-nisable motives and gestures of the translator, the translator whose 'saying again' was once promoted by the German Romantic philosophers above the claims and ambitions of analytic criticism. Clark, however, turns every which way in the effort not to succumb to the latter, including the direction of lyric poetry which must have been this book's chief fascination for me as I attempted to persuade my academic patrons that poetry could be, perhaps, a form of research, a means of getting beneath a painting's skin with effects – different, better? – from those of discursive prose.

On the evidence of Clark's study, poems about paintings may be the chief means of resisting such an idea. Clark offers little explicit comment on his turn to poetry in his study. What strikes one first is that very few of the poems are directly about the Poussin paintings in question. Some are dramatic monologues, one is a meditation on the role his art might have played in the life of his patron, Pointel. And when one of the poems does address a canvas directly it is followed immediately by a diary entry that expresses dissatisfaction with the poem's use of the word 'blue' to evoke the precise hue of a Poussin sky, even although the poem itself is concerned with such nuance.

In a sense, these poems look away from the paintings and into the stories and lives of the people associated with them, implying that poetry just cannot do the same work as paint even if it may illuminate, signal, enthuse in seductive verbal ways that may encourage readers to return and look again... and again, for that which the poem can't express. Clark himself is not so gloomy, at least not explicitly so. He is adamant at one point that he means to make poems. They are not simply a 'tactic' 'as steps towards a more flexible prose'. 'I do think a good poem about Poussin would be the highest form of criticism,' he writes, yet immediately worries about the nature and status of 'bad poems about paintings... What *is* it about the genre?' he asks. Clark's honesty is disarming and revealing. His poems, good as they are, are certainly strategic moves towards the creation of a prose which he fantasises as being 'light as a feather, fast as free association, exact and heavy as a fingerprint'. He turns back, constantly, from poetry to prose, and does he really want a poem about Poussin to be the highest form of criticism when it is, precisely, critical discourse that is found wanting in its approach to those elements in visual art that resist formulation in language?

Clark's originality is to have created a text that is neither a collection of poems nor an art history. It is not criticism or prose poetry. It is a mixture of all these elements and comes as close as anything I have ever read to giving us in language the life of a painting. I think now that I can pinpoint the moment in my own collection when this book's mode and message must have sunk in. My poems, like Clark's, often skirt around paintings and are more interested in story and incident. Often, despite my best endeavours, personal concerns and obsessions percolate through. And there is what seems now to be an inevitable turn towards prose, a flexible poetic prose that refuses the competing framing devices of lyric prosody and signals the inability of criticism to permit a sensuous submission to the picture's idiom.

And as the candle dwindles and my eyelids droop – no doubt yours as well, dear reader – I imagine the ideal shape of this collection and the word 'choreography' springs to mind. Perhaps, what happens here is a kind of joust or ballet as lyric poem cedes to prose poem or critical fragment, each one implying a certain dissatisfaction with its own mode of approach to canvas, installation, art film, a dissatisfaction thematised to some degree in John Bargrave's monologue that conjures balefully with notions of 'collection' and 'selection'. Is this pattern not that of research itself and have I not at least begun to discharge my obligations to my demanding patrons? As for the recurrence throughout the collection of images evoking smallness, the miniature, perhaps these can be traced to the presence in Poussin's paintings of tiny, sometimes barely perceptible figures, those placed as Clark puts it 'at the threshold between seeing and remembering', a dialectic at the very heart of visual art's uniqueness. The difficulty with this analysis is that it is just *that* and conducted – to boot – in bed! It is the rationalisation of a process that has been undertaken in states of intermittent consciousness. It would not be a book of poetry otherwise. Enough has been said, perhaps, to suggest why a 'critical preface' of the type promised is not possible and why I find myself at the end of this 'afterword' so grateful to M. de Norvins for allowing me to romance my predicament and ask the gentle reader's pardon.

One final question nags: the one asked by Clark of 'bad poems about paintings'. At the risk of giving hostages to fortune I shall hazard an answer. The exasperation we feel before bad ekphrastic art is simply an exacerbation of the disappointment we must feel before all poems about paintings, and maybe even before all poems and all paintings: we experience the mismatch of two entirely different worlds, the profound desire that pulls them into each other's orbits and we cry out that despite the ingenuity of each alien discourse the end result is a tense silence, a space across which each reaches and never meets; indeed the best image for this is perhaps the outstretched arm of the man running from corpse and snake in Poussin's painting, a space Clark tries and tries to put into words, concluding that it is the unnameable, the unsayable that is painting itself. Our only consolation, and it is a stimulating as well as a bleak one, is that the experience offered by ekphrasis focuses attention on the inadequate otherness of all art forms as they grapple with the real world they seek to represent.

Can we dream our way out of the impasse, or even finesse it just a little, by adapting the words Baudelaire used of his little poems in prose? Who among us has not, in his days of ambition, dreamt of the miracle of 'proem' or 'essoem', musical lines instinct with rhythm and echoing rhyme, both supple and sufficiently stravaiging to marry the bracing astringency of intellect to the upsurges of conscience and the unconscious, ready to subdue all of this to the modest and true passivity with which we must look and look again at the spectacle of the world.

A Cabinet of Curiosities

Passover

For I will consider my Cat Jeoffrey.
Christopher Smart

I will consider my imaginary cat.
For he is the servant of ambiguous truth
And is present in Tavistock Square
On the Number 30 bus.
He smiles in the sun with a Cheshire Cat smile.
For he is a brilliant theologian
And his electrical skin is the static
On handrails that pulley us up on deck.
He is the purring of traffic at lights.
He is the patience at the interminable stop.
There is nothing more gimlet-eyed
When he discerns the bodies,
The scattered bread, smashed bottles of wine,
Nothing more savoured, more teased at
In the cradle of his mind
Than this Passover of blood to lintel
And the stink of crucified hyssop.
For there is nothing more agitated
Than this Cherub Cat, this Angel Tiger,
Nothing more discerning than his imaginary
Question hissed to the hushed London hour:
'But which, my children, is Egypt?
And which is Israel?'

Three Gaelic Versions

On the Beach at Bosta
after Domhnall MacAmhlaigh

An old house decomposes
to my left;
sea is travelling
to my right.

Pitched up on my elbow
I make a kind of cavern
for the crab-coloured sand. It skitters
away to the edge of the inlet
where the sun pins it white,
irradiating the grains' faces –
faces which surfaced one day
between surges, gleamed and glanced
with the township's history.

Behind me is a garden;
under fallow hillocks
tucked away from the sun
the people are in history.
Facing its stones,
within sight of the roofless house
and the sea,
a world swings into its antipodes,
and history turns over and over and over.

poem/song/destiny
after Aonghas MacNeacail

you spraycanned my soul
with your heartcore bitch
graffiti when the wall ran out

crumbled into wee fritters
of cement and blue and red paint;
so you picked a brand new

john's syntaxoscopic interface;
he's already bulldozed
and your guff clings on eternally;

heat dogg, heartmonger, boy
bitch, you scuffed back earth
from ditch to ditch;

left me barking
as bad as your bite
and limp

but even if I harpooned my dick
I won't howk out your beauty
the spring spatter of your laughter

the palimpsest tattoo
left by your fingers
grindcore at my throat

your puckered evil
little flower
sucking up my face

The Crib
after Meg Bateman

A calm evening:
the empty sky sways
in the window's crib…
Hush love
and you will hear all the ghost words
moving westwards.

It is not the fair original
that makes me mawkish
(his subtle specificities)
but a life of desires,
every type of the god
abandoning me
for your sake, blond Gaelic Antony.

Listen with me,
until each bare-headed Celtic syllable
has stepped,
has rustled shingle-like out
through the grave stone walls.

They'll steer well clear,
mute as your sperm jumps within me
and the tears rent
by our version of the deed
will be as intense as the exquisite music
of that strange procession
when you emblazon it abroad.

The Hangingshaw

Then you sleep again and wake, begin the day.
Walking past the Hangingshaw, you notice
again how provisional the grass and bushes are

since they cleared the 'prefabs' so we could build
nothing there, how the space is still mapped out
in little plots where enamel sinks and mangels stood.

'*Hey bab-a-ree-bab, Ma mammy's got a prefab.*'
The rhyme doesn't linger but a man is lying
some way off in a patch of sunlight. He's too far

away to tell what's happened, but his suit
is visible and he's stretched out, arms by his side,
attention-like, right in the centre of a box-shaped green.

He seems peaceful and at home. Once, before
the prefabs, an anti-aircraft gun pounded the sky
from here; earlier still the Hangingshaw was just

a wood clinging to a hillside giving shade
to travellers. And historians dispute its
spelling for maybe it was Hagginshaw instead.

'*Hey bab-a-ree-bab*'. Later, in the night,
there is a dream with a friendly scuffle
in which your opponent suddenly turns

and embraces you: there is no pressure
of desire or want but an absolutely even
acceptance of you as you of him.

'I love you,' you say, the cushie-doos
return: '*Hey bab-a-ree-bab*', '*Hey bab-a-ree-bab*'
and you don't need to know what it might mean.

Reading at the Kibble Palace, Glasgow

for Richard Price

The poet kibbled among flowers: acanthus and lilac, the extremely unGlaswegian hosted beneath our palace of glass, twined to our iron buttresses and trellises. Under the dripping threshold of Botanic Gardens the poet launched his poems at us as we parked our bums in the very entrance way to Eden. And his quiet voice gathered them, infallibly, gathered the people to the previously quiet lychgate to the flowers; as if he had unlocked the trees, unbraided the long ears of the palms and now folk could walk past, past the poet's words and use them to step in, lie or sit on benches and eat their noisy lunch-box apples. Pigeons shuffled the roof above his head, dealing his words to the air, to the children's cries which took them up and trumped them with their own. All the people passed him, indifferent, embarrassed, apologetic, smiling, stony-faced, indignant, but each pocketed, each snuck up a word as he sidestepped them in mid-flight: 'trout are influential', 'aquaflora', of course, caught like burrs on the double buggy's wheels as it pushed weans towards the greenery. 'A hem of air' stitched a down-and-out's frayed hems and the name 'Fiona' savoured the lips of a royally built black woman who tossed it back to you with nonchalant contempt. They were there, the people, not listening to you but listening as their bodies took the imprint of that awkwardness where language washed like a sea taken from its element and dashed about the Kibble's deck. Later they'll remember the day they dodged your words to make their rendezvous with plants, faced down poems to make their tryst with fronds. Not that they'll thank you but they'll think about language and it will thank them for you.

Second Poem of the Hip Bone

after the French of Jean Sénac

1

A Rainbow Wrasse a little shade and the promise of glances
Here our halt
In a savage stretch of sun.
From one rock to another, from one dune
To a corner of the harbour wall
Syllables pursue each other, words assemble, the book
Blossoms.
Wide-eyed, my breath in me as tasty as seafood,
I do my lines of summer vocab.

2

And the word
Like an effusion of water
Takes the form of our bodies.
Writing becomes
A vertiginous anatomy
(With all the risks of embolism
And the patient pleasure of un-
Covering beneath your lips
Earth-covered sense).

3

I love writing because
Its caress covers you,
Naming your flesh in its most ferocious otherness,
Drinking even from our very dreams,
With the same purified mouth,
Those words mad with sun and blood orange!

4

From me to me you are
The smile that leads to secret forges.

Armed in your marine spectacles
And blue harpoon,
You take all the aggressive words prisoner.
In the evening, we light a kelp fire on the sand
And you dance with only a word on.

The Mocking Fairy

after a pen and ink drawing by Hannah Frank

And out of her cold cottage never answered Mrs. Gill
The Fairy mimbling, mambling in the garden.
                                Walter de la Mare, 'The Mocking Fairy'

This is the house that Hannah built,
one window lit, one window dark,
dark as the forest made of pen and ink
and the fairy mimbling, mambling in the garden.

A mocking, whispering aphid, this fairy
is vaguely anorexic, a line of arms and legs
that grows from trees scored up in black
whose sap is virgin paper, a wing-like translucence

tough as rope. One star falls beneath
the constellations, lower even than the moon,
falling on the grass of fallen stars
past the creeper that was human.

The house that Hannah built is odd:
symmetry suggests two windows,
three perhaps, with one behind the tree;
the unlit one peeks out, maimed but dark

against the mimbling, mambling in the garden.
Mrs Gill is there within the house;
can she hear the fairy from the lit
or unlit room? Would she cry out

in the small hours or at dawn?
Words are curling in the margins
at the paper's edge and the fairy
feels them mimble mamble through her toes.

Mrs Gill is lit and unlit, star and tree,
rope of ink and moon and wing;
she flits between her virgin rooms
always on the brink of speech;

and out of her cold cottage never answered Mrs. Gill
the Fairy mimbling, mambling in the garden.

The Organ Bath

for Alison Gurney

Just as you record the ions flowing
through lung membrane strung
between the test tubes of an 'organ bath',
so I encourage electron transport
across the gap junction of connected words
and amplify the current linking them:
imagine flooding 'organ' with 'Lucifer
Yellow', a fluorescent dye that illuminates
the evanescent footprint of warm air
among the pathways of the body;
the word lights up and all its associations
sing as Ion did to Socrates: 'reed organ'
conducts you to the 'organ-pipe cactus',
'organ-pipe coral' but some organs
are just more lovable than others,
above them all the Steam Calliope,
named for 'the fair voiced' muse of epic poetry,
whose tiny knurled wheels inked rollers up
with sound and kept the Mississippi riverboats
in fine, full-throated voice. Implements,
musical instruments, organs of the body
leviathan the flood which pours down
from the Indo-European *worg*
and gave Greek 'ergon' meaning 'work'.
This is our work, our 'organ bath':
'work immersed in water, in mud',
the world, the body, the poem
breathed through the lungs of language,
steaming out its Calliope songs.

Sailing to Torcello

A Doge of work! The scrolls, the endless
parchments of middle age! Applications and appeals
blot out the throb of bells, suppress
the smell of dust and hot cowhide, the peals
of youthful laughter and dismiss
the fact that rose gold sky is still held up by angels.
He doodles briefly, sighs; only a fresco, a cartoon
by Titian could show all flesh sinking in this salt lagoon.

A glorified skivvy with a pointy hat, he tackles
the intractable while all the others trade and trade
even though each year the ramshackle
world they hedge and bet is weighed
in balances by bankers whose chuckles,
crackles, heckles are commissioned and ignored.
And so he takes the vaporetto
to the holy island of Torcello.

Meter Theu! Mother of God! No Doge can save
you, long, sleek and blue in your high iconostasis.
Gabriel hastens but is not quick enough; Eve
kneels, is not forgiven. Even, especially, this oasis
is the first to go: apostles in the nave
of meadows, trampled poppies in the still mosaic.
The boy locked in his almond shell will have to swim.
Cloth for earth is in the Doge's hymn.

'Star of the seas!', he prays, 'Epitome of virtue;
the skies are starless and a severed peacock's tail
floats by, fans out its single iridescent eye to view
mens' wisdom, giving up on God. Soft braille
of feathers, drowned lions, is it true
that heaven only lay beneath us among the kale
and sandbanks? The canals all run with fire.
Gold endures but we are out of art and nature.

Edwin Morgan is eating an orange

Edwin Morgan is eating an orange.
'Tasty, zesty orange,' he mutters.

Edwin Morgan folds the segments back
and shrinks to the size of a pip.

Edwin Morgan cradles each piece of peel
in the small of his bony hand.

Edwin Morgan steps into the orange
and zips up the liths behind him.

Edwin Morgan's taxi driver
and Edwin Morgan's interviewer
step into Edwin Morgan's room.

The journalist lurches off again,
mystified, disappointed,
and the taxi driver pockets an orange.

Notes

'Five Portraits of Mary': Mary, Queen of Scots was herself a poet and knew the great Renaissance French poet Pierre de Ronsard, who may have tutored her. Examples of her embroidery are still extant. John Acheson became Master of the Mint around 1558. The ivory carving that forms the subject of 'Family' may be viewed in the local museum on the island of Korkula in Croatia.

'Resisting Hell': Esther Inglis (married name Kello; 1571–1624) was a miniaturist, calligrapher, embroiderer, translator and writer. Of Huguenot origin, her family escaped to Scotland to avoid persecution. Her father became Master of the French School in Edinburgh.

'To a Gentleman of the King's Bedchamber': this is based on letters from the 3rd Earl of Lothian, William Kerr to his father the Earl of Ancram. Kerr signed the Scottish national covenant in 1638, took part in the march into England in 1640 and fought at the Battle of Newburn. Despite being on opposite sides in the Civil War, father and son maintained their correspondence. Kerr also collected paintings and used John Clerk of Penicuik as an agent on the European art markets of the day.

'Rousseau on Ramsay': Alan Ramsay's portraits of Jean-Jacques Rousseau, author of *Les Confessions*, and David Hume used to hang in Hume's living room, despite his famous quarrel with the Frenchman.

'Young Blade': combines scenes from two paintings, one by Henry Raeburn of *The Reverend Robert Walker Skating on Duddingston Loch* and another by Charles Lees showing members of a skating club on the same loch by moonlight. Some years ago a minor controversy was ignited when it was suggested that the author of the painting of Walker might not have been Raeburn but a Frenchman named Danloux.

'Sir David Wilkie Administering Tea in Kensington': the young Delacroix met Wilkie in London in 1825. Delacroix is on record as saying he preferred Wilkie's gifts as a draughtsman to his skill as a painter.

'Sleuth': the setting is the Hôtel Chevillon in the village of Grez situated on the River Loing, a few kilometres south of Fontainebleau. Better known for hosting Robert Louis Stevenson who met his wife Fanny Osbourne there, Chevillon lodged large numbers of artists throughout the latter half of the nineteenth century, including figures such as Corot, Arthur Melville, Carl Larsson, August Strindberg and John Lavery. Comte Henri de Lestrange was a real photographer and his pictures of the Fontainebleau area may be seen at the Bibliothèque Nationale. He was an amateur and nothing much is known about him. The poem draws on ideas presented in Serge Tisseron's study *Le Mystère de la Chambre Claire* (Paris: Flammarion, 1996).

'Disruption': the pioneer photographer and painter David Octavius Hill (1802–70) was present when, in 1843, the Church of Scotland split and 450 ministers left to form the Free Church of Scotland. Hill used the new invention of photography to make likenesses of all those present, later converting them over a period of twenty-three years into the portraits in the enormous canvas depicting the event. Duncan MacMillan suggests in his history of Scottish painting that the French Revolutionary painter David influenced Hill, particularly his work showing the first meeting of the Estates General at the Jeu de Paume in Paris. Hill's work is the focus of an excellent book on the subject by John Fowler, *Mr Hill's Big Picture* (Edinburgh: Saint Andrew Press, 2006).

'Lob': Sir John Lavery (1856–1941), after education in Glasgow and Paris and a spell painting *plein-air* in Grez-sur-Loing, returned to Glasgow in 1885 and painted *The Tennis Party*, set in a field beside the River Cart. Jacques Henri Lartigue (1894–1986), French photographer famous for his photos of tennis and other sporting occasions.

'In the rue Annette': Sir David Young Cameron (1865–1945), painter and particularly fine etcher.

'A Backward Glance': Charles Rennie Mackintosh (1868–1928) had given up his career as an architect by 1923. Towards the end of his life he and his wife Margaret MacDonald (1865–1933) moved to Port Vendres, near Perpignan, where he devoted his time to water-colour painting.

'Between the Lines': F.C.B. Cadell (1883–1937) was one of the group of painters now known collectively as the Scottish Colourists. Other members were Guy Peploe, (1871–1935), J.D. Fergusson (1874–1961) and Leslie Hunter (1877–1931).

'The Place de L'Institut': Anne Redpath (1895–1965) had a long association with France, living and painting there on many occasions.

'Helping with an Enquiry': Robert Colquhoun (1914–62) and Robert MacBryde (1913–1966), the 'two Roberts' as they're sometimes known, both born in Ayrshire, met at Glasgow School of Art and achieved a measure of fame in London during the 1940s with Expressionist work and still lifes. Members of a loose circle of friends that included John Minton and Francis Bacon, they managed to live fairly openly as a gay couple despite the times. A friend destroyed some of Colquhoun's erotic work after his death fearing the consequences of a police enquiry into a party that went awry.

'Small Pleasures': Ian Hamilton Finlay's work is best appreciated by visiting his garden at Little Sparta, Dunsyre, just south of Edinburgh. Yves Abrioux's book on Finlay, *A Visual Primer* (London: Reaktion Books, 1994) is a beautiful record of his work. The doll-sized versions of Mackintosh's work referred to here are by Michael and Margaret Hartley.

'Finger of a Frenchman': John Bargrave (1610–80) is the subject of a remarkable study by Stephen Bann: *Under the Sign* (Ann Arbor: University of Michigan Press, 1995). Jonathan Sawday's *The Body Emblazoned: Dissection and the Human Body in Renaissance Culture* (London: Routledge, 1996) was a fascinating and helpful resource. The cento towards the end of the poem reworks famous lines by the seventeenth-century poet Thomas Traherne, from his *Centuries of Meditations* (Third Century, Section 3).

'After Words, After Art': T.J. Clark, *The Sight of Death: An Experiment in Art Writing* (New Haven: Yale University Press, 2006).